Teaching Architecture(s) in the Post-Covid Era

In the post-COVID era, understanding the profound impact of digital technologies on design pedagogy is crucial. This book delves into experimental design education, showcasing projects utilising technology to transform creative and analytical processes.

Emphasising the potential for digital-era technologies to create novel educational opportunities, the book addresses recent global events and their role in minimising educational disruptions in the evolving hybrid educational landscape. Each chapter offers case studies exploring digital technology's influence across architectural education, spanning interior design, urban planning, parametric digital design, architectural conservation, and design analysis. Contributors envision the hybrid virtual design studio's future and discuss the collaborative role of digital technologies in urban design projects. The book analyses contemporary parametric design processes and machine learning through innovative historical case studies, examining new technologies in architectural conservation.

With case studies from diverse locations, including South Africa, Turkey, the UK, and the United States, the book provides a global perspective on the influences and potential futures of digital technologies in architecture. Essential for those interested in the future of spatial design education, this book illuminates the pivotal role of technology in shaping its trajectory.

Sadiyah Geyer has over a decade of industry expertise and excels in executing interior architecture and design projects. Specialising in conceptual development, technical documentation, and project management, she brings a deep passion for creating spaces that enhance society with minimal environmental impact. Currently an academic and researcher at the University of Johannesburg, Sadiyah shares her knowledge with aspiring interior designers. Her rewarding teaching experience spans seven years. Recently commencing a PhD journey, she focuses on urban regeneration strategies and the role of interior design in shaping urban interiority, building on her MA (Design) qualification from the University of Johannesburg.

Routledge Focus on Design Pedagogy
Series Editor: Graham Cairns

The Routledge Focus on Design Pedagogy series provides the reader with the latest scholarship for instructors who educate designers. The series publishes research from across the globe and covers areas as diverse as beginning design and foundational design, architecture, product design, interior design, fashion design, landscape architecture, urban design, and architectural conservation and historic preservation. By making these studies available to the worldwide academic community, the series aims to promote quality design education.

Fluid Space and Transformational Learning
Kyriaki Tsoukala

Progressive Studio Pedagogy
Examples from Architecture and Allied Design Fields
Edited by Charlie Smith

Emerging Practices in Architectural Pedagogy
Accommodating an Uncertain Future
Edited by Laura Sanderson and Sally Stone

Teaching Architecture(s) in the Post-Covid Era
The New Age of Digital Design
Edited by Sadiyah Geyer

For more information about this series, please visit: https://www.routledge.com/architecture/series/RFDP

Teaching Architecture(s) in the Post-Covid Era
The New Age of Digital Design

Edited by Sadiyah Geyer

LONDON AND NEW YORK

First published 2024
by Routledge
4 Park Square, Milton Park, Abingdon, Oxon OX14 4RN

and by Routledge
605 Third Avenue, New York, NY 10158

Routledge is an imprint of the Taylor & Francis Group, an informa business

© 2024 selection and editorial matter, Sadiyah Geyer; individual chapters, the contributors

The right of Sadiyah Geyer to be identified as the author of the editorial material, and of the authors for their individual chapters, has been asserted in accordance with sections 77 and 78 of the Copyright, Designs and Patents Act 1988.

All rights reserved. No part of this book may be reprinted or reproduced or utilised in any form or by any electronic, mechanical, or other means, now known or hereafter invented, including photocopying and recording, or in any information storage or retrieval system, without permission in writing from the publishers.

Trademark notice: Product or corporate names may be trademarks or registered trademarks, and are used only for identification and explanation without intent to infringe.

British Library Cataloguing-in-Publication Data
A catalogue record for this book is available from the British Library

Library of Congress Cataloging-in-Publication Data
Names: Geyer, Sadiyah, editor.
Title: Teaching architecture(s) in the post-Covid era : the new age of digital design / [editor] Sadiyah Geyer.
Other titles: Teaching architecture in the post-Covid era
Description: Abingdon, Oxon : Routledge, 2025. | Series: Routledge focus on design pedagogy | Includes bibliographical references and index.
Identifiers: LCCN 2024011212 (print) | LCCN 2024011213 (ebook) | ISBN 9781032564104 (hardback) | ISBN 9781032564135 (paperback) | ISBN 9781003435396 (ebook)
Subjects: LCSH: Architecture--Study and teaching--Technological innovations. | Educational technology.
Classification: LCC NA2000 .T43 2025 (print) | LCC NA2000 (ebook) | DDC 720.71--dc23/eng/20240325
LC record available at https://lccn.loc.gov/2024011212
LC ebook record available at https://lccn.loc.gov/2024011213

ISBN: 978-1-032-56410-4 (hbk)
ISBN: 978-1-032-56413-5 (pbk)
ISBN: 978-1-003-43539-6 (ebk)

DOI: 10.4324/9781003435396

Typeset in Times New Roman
by KnowledgeWorks Global Ltd.

Contents

List of Figures vi
List of Contributors ix

Introduction 1
SADIYAH GEYER

1 **The Augmented Studio: Teaching and Learning in Digital Space** 9
REBECCA DISNEY, NAOMI HOUSE, AND FRANCESCA MURIALDO

2 **Digital Twin Cities: An Instrument for Pedagogical Change** 25
CALAYDE DAVEY

3 **Poorly Trained: Towards an AI Pedagogy in Architecture** 56
JEAN JAMINET, GABRIEL ESQUIVEL, AND SHANE BUGNI

4 **A Point Cloud Pedagogy** 78
ROBERT STEPNOSKI

5 **Observing/Performing the (Pandemic) Every Day: Photographic Writing as a Curating Tool in Online Architectural Education** 101
BILGE BERIL KAPUSUZ BALCI

Index 120

Figures

1.1	Interior Architecture at Middlesex University.	14
1.2	The Expanded Studio/Interaction and Interaction.	16
1.3	The Expanded Studio – The Modelmaking Workshops.	16
1.4	The Expanded Studio – The Global Classroom.	17
1.5	The Augmented Studio – A Manifesto.	20
2.1	The Hatfield Digital Twin City is approximately twenty-square-kilometre digital development area in South Africa.	33
2.2	Coupling foreground digital twin city development activities directly to background learning activities, students were tasked to map formal and informal South African urban areas through OpenStreetMap.	35
2.3	Foreground education meets digital city development, as students create two improved transportation designs in two days, leveraging their shared digital intelligence.	37
2.4	The complex and fast-paced urban growth of the Melusi informal settlement.	39
2.5	The open GIS mapping results from the 2022 Informal Settlement Climate Adaption Studio.	40
2.6	Exam project outcomes from chemical engineering students working with the architecture department on urban topics using digital twin city data for AI/ML training.	42
2.7	Transdisciplinary shared digital learning to create digital twin city geometric data works.	43
2.8	Building open GIS spatial histories for fast-changing informal urban environments.	45
2.9	Student design responses for 2022 Melusi Climate Adaption Studio.	46
3.1	Distorted figures in a diptych of portraits by Francis Bacon. In Bacon's portrait of a male subject (left), diagrammatic interruptions appear as black colour patches that distort facial features. Bacon's depiction of a female figure (right) modulates facial features with amorphous shadows and bold brush strokes.	59

Figures vii

3.2 Similar "scrambled zones" visible in AI-generated faces. The machine learning process produces similar "scrambled zones" that distort the facial features of a male figure (left). Similar diagrammatic interruptions are visible in an AI-generated face of a female subject resembling Bacon's portraits (right). 59
3.3 GAN architecture diagram by authors. 60
3.4 Poor training process diagram for a sample of Serlio's columns by authors. 63
3.5 StyleGAN image distortions by Brenden Bjerke (left) and Nate Gonzalez (right). 65
3.6 Representation of voxel stacking and ultraviolet (UV) mapping by John Scott. 66
3.7 CT scans (left) and encoded patterns (right) by John Scott. 67
3.8 Models created through voxel stacking by John Scott (left) and Luis Sanabria (right). 68
3.9 Style transfer output (left) and rewrapped morphed object (right) by John Scott. 68
3.10 StyleGAN distortion (left) and sinGAN fragmentation (right) by Spencer Young. 69
3.11 High- and low-fidelity components (left) form an eroded artefact (right) by Spencer Young. 70
3.12 Style transfer output (left) and rewrapped vermiculated form (right) by Spencer Young. 70
3.13 Encoded pattern (left) and voxel-stacked object with solid windows (right) by Erin Carter. 72
3.14 Models created through voxel stacking (left) and decomposition technique (right) by Erin Carter. 72
3.15 Morphological assembly (right) with hyper-articulated decoration that appears as esoteric glyphs (left) by Austin White. 73
4.1 Dual flight path for best image overlap. Class: Reality Capture for Architecture, University of Texas at Austin, School of Architecture. 89
4.2 Tie Points. Class: Reality Capture for Architecture, University of Texas at Austin, School of Architecture. 90
4.3 Spheres representing 3D laser scanner locations. Class: Reality Capture for Architecture, University of Texas at Austin, School of Architecture. 91
4.4 Centre oculus using gradated collage. Class: Reality Capture for Architecture, University of Texas at Austin, School of Architecture. 92
4.5 Internal tower of the stair tower chamber. Class: Reality Capture for Architecture, University of Texas at Austin, School of Architecture. 93

viii *Figures*

4.6	Reverse view of internal tower. Class: Reality Capture for Architecture, University of Texas at Austin, School of Architecture.	93
4.7	Schematic drawing section. Class: Reality Capture for Architecture, University of Texas at Austin, School of Architecture.	95
4.8	Subterranean chambers. Class: Reality Capture for Architecture, University of Texas at Austin, School of Architecture.	96
4.9	Building C, loops of images. Class: Reality Capture for Architecture, University of Texas at Austin, School of Architecture.	97
5.1	Phase 1: Cure for the self: "The Square: The Heart" by Zeynep Coşkuner.	109
5.2	Exhibition poster and the digital exhibition environment.	111
5.3	Phase 2: Cure for the City: "Confusion" by Hüseyin Avni Halıcı.	111
5.4	Phase 2: Cure for the City: "The Square: The Heart" by Zeynep Coşkuner.	112
5.5	Phase 2: Cure for the City: "Crossroads" by Eren Burak Çöplü.	113
5.6	Phase 2: Cure for the city: "Mirror mirror on the wall who is the fastest city of them all?" by Dilannur Özdemir.	113
5.7	Phase 2: Cure for the City: "Gap" by Yaşanur Çil.	114

Contributors

Shane Bugni is a junior at Texas A&M University, where he is pursuing a bachelor's degree in architecture. He studies the integration of artificial neural networks into contemporary architectural workflows. Shane has served as a technology assistant for courses in artificial intelligence and robotic fabrication at Texas A&M University.

Calayde Davey, PhD in Environmental Design, Economics and Planning, and a South African Architecture Master's, brings a diverse international career spanning architecture, Lean construction management, and urban planning. As a project architect in Southeast Asia and a Lean facilitator for the largest Passive House project in the United States, she co-authored "Mastering Lean Leadership." Currently co-chairing Lean Built Environment Afrika, Davey directs Regen50 – Urban Strategies. Engaged in a post-doctoral research project on African Digital Twin Cities, she teaches at various universities, shaping the future of the African built environment sector.

Rebecca Disney, MA RCA FHEA, is a versatile designer and educator, transitioning from bespoke furniture and lighting design to impactful interior spaces. Collaborating with Lanyon-Hogg Architects on diverse projects, including hotel refurbishments and commercial spaces, she recently contributed to a North London music rehearsal space. As a Senior Lecturer in Interior Architecture Design at Middlesex University, Rebecca explores affective reasoning in design processes, focusing on strategies and tactics within interior and architectural spaces. Her work has been featured in Interior Educators' platform IE: Studio Issue#4, and her study "Affective Reasoning: Hidden Interiors" was part of the 2021 Practice-based Outputs REF UoA32 at Middlesex University.

Gabriel Esquivel was educated as an architect in Mexico City with a degree from the National University and received a master's degree in architecture from The Ohio State University. Gabriel is the director of the T4T Lab at Texas A&M University, where he examines the integration of digital

x Contributors

technology to exchange architectural information and its connection to contemporary theory.

Naomi House, a designer, educator, and writer, is a Senior Lecturer in Interior Architecture and Design at Middlesex University. Specialising in the psycho-spatial dimension of interiors, her research challenges the resistance to change in domestic interiors. With expertise in forensic methods, Naomi explores how objects and environments shape daily behaviours. Formerly at the Royal College of Art and Chelsea College of Art, she has tutored at London Metropolitan University and University College London. Currently, Naomi serves as an External Examiner for interior design programmes at Regents University and the Glasgow School of Art and is a member of Middlesex University's Unity of Assessment 32 for the Research Excellence Framework (UoA32 REF) Committee.

Jean Jaminet holds a Master of Architecture from Princeton University and a Bachelor of Science in Architecture from The Ohio State University. He is currently an assistant professor at Kent State University, where he conducts design and research that examines the perception of the built environment influenced by our fundamental reliance on technology.

Dr. Bilge Beril Kapusuz Balci is an Assistant Professor at Gazi University Department of Architecture, where she teaches architectural design, exhibition histories, and architectural photography. Her research focuses on architectural theory, urban history, theory and history of photography, and microhistories of architectural exhibitions and publications. She completed her PhD in Architecture in 2018 with a dissertation on the historical archives of the Venice Biennale. Recently, she conducted postdoctoral research at the Iuav University of Venice, exploring critical pedagogies of architectural photography in the 1970s as a fellow of The Scientific and Technological Research Council of Turkey.

Francesca Murialdo, BA, MSc (Hons), PhD, Senior Fellow of Advance HE (SFHEA), serves as the Programme Leader for Interior Architecture at Middlesex University, London. An architect with a PhD in Interior Architecture and Exhibition Design, she has taught and practised interiors since 1998. Her research focuses on spatial connections, emphasising emerging behaviours and strategies. Francesca has lectured globally, founded practices Studiometrico and Labomint, and earned recognitions such as ArchDaily's Building of the Year in 2009. Co-director of Interior Educators and Director for Research at European Interior Educators, she boasts a substantial publication record in research and practice.

Robert Stepnoski is a Senior Lecturer and Remote Pilot at the University of Texas at Austin and studied Architecture at the Architectural Center in Boston, Massachusetts. His current research focuses on leveraging Unmanned

Aerial Vehicles (UAVs) for mapping and modelling, paired with Information Technologies, particularly in Historic Preservation Documentation. With his latest class, "Reality Capture for Architecture," Stepnoski explores three levels of 3D scanning and photogrammetry technology, emphasising UAV-generated aerial photography and video capture. Additionally, he investigates UAVs' potential in aiding first responders and mapping evolving flood plains, highlighting their ability to access disaster-affected areas safely.

Introduction

Sadiyah Geyer

While digital design tools have been informing design education significantly in recent decades, the COVID-19 pandemic took their impact to a new level. Today, in the post-COVID era, it is thus fundamental that we assess just how much, and in what ways, "the digital" currently informs the nature of design pedagogy. Within this context, this book explores the experimental fringes of design education through projects that are currently using technology to aid, reshape, and deconstruct the creative design and analytical process. It argues that digital-era technologies can create new design educational opportunities and, considered in the light of recent global events, also identifies how they can help reduce educational disruptions in what will be an increasingly hybrid educational future.

Each chapter presents a case study related to how various digital technologies are influencing the full range of architectural education fields, including interior design, urban planning, parametric digital design, architectural conservation, and architectural design. Its authors consider the role of technologies in creating the hybrid virtual design studio of the future and the nature of education within that setting. They discuss the role of the digital in collaborative education and practice projects in urban design and planning, and they offer an analysis of contemporary parametric design processes and related machine learning through an innovative historical case study. In addition, the book's authors examine the new technologies being applied in the field of architectural conservation and the future of photography and drawing as an increasingly digital tool in the increasingly hybrid (digital and physical) setting of architectural education.

Bringing together case studies from South Africa, Turkey, the UK, and the United States, the book not only presents a sample of the diversity of influences and potential futures for digital technologies in the broad field of architecture but it will also do so with global perspectives. Through the book, readers embark on an interconnected journey through five chapters that collectively explore the transformative landscape of education in the digital age. Chapter 1 looks at the future of the hybrid design studio pedagogy through the lens of interior design. In Chapter 2, we move on to urban planning education

DOI: 10.4324/9781003435396-1

using shared digital twinning methodologies that use technology to connect education with practice with a case study from South Africa. From there, Chapter 3 moves into the realm of parametric design with an examination of the "mechanics" of artificial intelligence (AI) learning involved in parametricism via a unique historical case study of Sebastiano Serlio's drawings. Introducing ideas that flow into Chapter 4, we then move onto a text that opens up perspectives on the role of digital technologies in contemporary architectural preservation through a chapter on point cloud technologies, photogrammetry, and 3D laser scanning. To close, the book returns in Chapter 5 to the design studio but this time through the lens of digital photography examined specifically in a case study set in the virtual teaching realm of COVID-19.

While we do not wish to rehearse all the arguments put forward by our authors, it will help the reader here if we offer a few pointers to each of the chapters in more detail. In Chapter 1, The Augmented Studio: Teaching and Learning in Digital Space by Rebecca Disney, Naomi House, and Francesca Murialdo, we have a text in which the authors suggest that the 21st century has witnessed an unprecedented digital revolution that fundamentally reshaped how we live, work, and communicate. Nowhere is this transformation more evident than in the realm of education. The convergence of technology and pedagogy has ushered in a new era of learning, challenging traditional paradigms and opening exciting possibilities for educators and learners alike. Disney, House, and Francesca Murialdo embark on a journey through the multifaceted landscape of digital education, exploring the seismic shifts brought about by the global COVID-19 pandemic and the subsequent embrace of digital tools and platforms. They delve into the transformative concepts of the "Expanded Studio" and the "Augmented Studio," which emerged as responses to the challenges and opportunities presented by the digital age.

In 2020, the world faced an unprecedented crisis as the COVID-19 pandemic swept across the globe, disrupting every facet of society, including education. Overnight, physical classrooms closed, and educators were compelled to adapt swiftly to remote teaching and online learning environments. This abrupt shift marked the beginning of a profound digital revolution in education, forcing educators to rethink their approaches, redefine their methods, and reimagine the essence of teaching and learning. As traditional boundaries between physical and digital learning spaces blurred, innovative educational paradigms took root. The "Expanded Studio" emerged as an adaptive solution, transcending the limitations of conventional pedagogies. It not only weathered the storm of the pandemic but also laid the groundwork for a new era of collaborative and digitally enhanced learning experiences.

Technology has long promised to revolutionise education, promising the prospect of democratising knowledge and fostering global connectivity. However, it has also unveiled the stark disparities in access to digital resources, posing challenges to equitable education for all. Disney, House, and Murialdo navigate the intricate terrain of these technological advancements, examining how digital tools and platforms intersect with pedagogy, culture, and society. They delve into the emerging field of digital anthropology, offering insights into the evolving dynamics of digital technologies and their profound impact on education.

At the forefront of this digital transformation stands the concept of the "Metaverse." Rooted in science fiction and powered by cutting-edge technologies such as blockchain, augmented and virtual reality, and AI, the Metaverse envisions a reality where the boundaries between physical and virtual worlds dissolve. It promises a future where learners seamlessly transition between digital and physical realms, expanding the horizons of educational possibilities.

As the authors embark on this exploration of the educational frontier, they confront profound questions about the nature of learning, the role of educators, and the evolving landscape of knowledge dissemination. The "Augmented Studio" thus emerges as a manifesto for a future pedagogy that embraces technology's potential to revolutionise education, with the authors navigating this dynamic landscape, uncovering the challenges, innovations, and limitless opportunities that await in this brave new world of digital education.

In Chapter 2, Digital Twin Cities: An Instrument for Pedagogical Change, Calayde Davey explores the concept of digital twin cities and offers a groundbreaking approach to revolutionising urban planning, design, and management. These digital replicas of physical cities, constructed through real-time data integration, hold immense potential for enhancing the sustainability and overall quality of urban life. However, their adoption faces several challenges, including the need for shared digital intelligence, digital skills, and robust data governance. The digital talent gap is a critical concern within the built environment industry, which has been further exacerbated by the COVID-19 pandemic. Despite the essential role of digital skills in ensuring future growth, the industry has been slow in embracing innovation and digital competencies, posing significant risks to its competitiveness and sustainability.

Davey emphasises the pivotal role that educators can play in addressing the digital talent gap by incorporating digital twin city development processes into core curricula. By reframing digital twin city development as a platform for digital training, educators can potentially equip students with the necessary skills for the digital era while benefiting local communities. The importance of developing a skilled workforce is underscored, as failure to invest in digital skills and talent may lead to the built environment industry falling behind in the adoption of emerging technologies.

Davey also highlights that addressing the digital talent gap requires a coordinated effort among educational institutions, employers, and industry stakeholders. It points out that the absence of digital competence as a shared core skill in built environment education, along with a lack of shared multidisciplinary digital training environments, contributes to the widening digital talent gap. Digital Twin Cities: An Instrument for Pedagogical Change concludes by emphasising that digital twin cities offer a unique opportunity to advance digital skills and create collaborative training environments within the built environment industry. Lessons from the Hatfield Digital Twin City Initiative serve as a valuable roadmap for other cities and industries aiming to embrace digital technologies and bridge the digital skills gap. The project, located in the City of Tshwane, South Africa, serves as a real-time urban laboratory employing digital twin technology to improve urban systems and processes. While facing challenges related to data quality, accessibility, and technical barriers, this initiative has adopted innovative, inclusive, and transdisciplinary approaches to foster digital literacy and skill development among students. It promotes a culture of collaboration and ongoing learning, ultimately preparing individuals for the digital demands of urban development and sustainability in the 21st century.

In Chapter 3, Poorly Trained: Towards an AI Pedagogy in Architecture, Jean Jaminet, Gabriel Esquivel, and Shane Bugni discuss the convergence of classical architectural treatises and modern machine-learning technologies representing a captivating intersection of tradition and innovation. This research endeavour embarks on a compelling journey into the world of Italian Mannerist architect Sebastiano Serlio's illustrated expositions. Through the transformative lens of AI, this exploration seeks to unveil the hidden parallels between Serlio's representational codes within his drawings and the intricate information processing mechanisms of contemporary AI systems.

The crux of this investigation is situated within the intriguing tension between analogue and digital information processing, symbolic of the ongoing dialogue between machine learning and architectural intelligence. Rather than offering straightforward, recognisable building simulations, this research dives into the realm of poorly trained AI models and enigmatic digital workflows. These deliberately misaligned creations defy conventional translations from drawings to tangible structures, reshaping the discourse that has characterised architecture since the Renaissance.

Jaminet, Esquivel, and Bugni's academic journey finds additional dimension through a series of thought-provoking visual experiments conducted during a design seminar at Texas A&M University. The seminar's unique blend of students from diverse architectural and engineering backgrounds served as fertile ground for creative collaborations, fostering a shared intelligence at the intersection of technology and creativity. In this unconventional learning environment, traditional student-professor interactions were artfully combined with machine learning experiments, leading to the cultivation of a low-fidelity design intelligence.

Deeper into the chapter, we encounter the influential role of the architectural treatise in shaping the discipline over time. Serlio's pioneering work, "All the Works on Architecture and Perspective," with its copious drawings and illustrations, is a testament to the fusion of visual and textual elements within this technical-literary genre. Serlio's journey is marked by his establishment of architectural codes, particularly the canonical five orders, which, paradoxically, he both adhered to and deviated from in his creations. This nuanced exploration underscores the profound connection between architectural language and the modulation of its codes, hinting at profound implications for the AI-driven architectural discourse.

Furthermore, Jaminet, Esquivel, and Bugni delve into the intricate interplay between analogical and digital modes of communication within language. Drawing from Gilles Deleuze's insights, it becomes clear that language itself is a result of this discordant pairing, giving rise to the function of the diagram as a modulator of meaning and representation. The diagram serves as a key to understanding the blurred boundaries between analogue and digital languages, further emphasising the aesthetic potential of these hybrid forms.

In parallel to Deleuze's theories, the chapter establishes intriguing parallels between the diagrammatic modulation observed in Francis Bacon's paintings and the transformations wrought by machine learning networks. Both realms produce novel effects, disrupting established conventions and challenging perceptions of representation. This parallel extends to the creative potential of generative adversarial networks (GANs), which, when poorly trained, yield images that defy categorisation and evoke alternative forms of visual intelligence.

The exploration reaches its apex in the description of a comprehensive experiment conducted within the design seminar. This experiment unfolds in three stages: dataset curation, layered GANs, and integrated parametric three-dimensionalisation. Through these stages, the study dissects the translation of Serlio's columns from 2D drawings to complex 3D forms, highlighting the transformational power of machine learning in reshaping architectural language and representation.

In conclusion, Jaminet, Esquivel, and Bugni embark on a transformative journey that traverses centuries of architectural tradition to converge with the cutting-edge realm of AI. The chapter invites readers to contemplate the intricate interplay between analogue and digital modes of communication, the potential of poorly trained AI models, and the transformative power of the diagram in reshaping our understanding of architecture. As we navigate this dynamic intersection, we discover that Serlio's illustrated volumes serve as a fertile ground for reimagining contemporary aesthetics, communication modes, and creative production through the lens of AI.

In Chapter 4, A Point Cloud Pedagogy by Robert Stepnoski, we enter the realm of architectural and historical exploration, where the fusion of advanced technology and time-honoured craftsmanship has yielded profound insights into the past. This fusion has revitalised the study of historic sites, enabling scholars and students to transcend traditional research boundaries. The narrative that follows embarks on an engaging journey guided by a group of dedicated students who embrace a pioneering exploration of historic sites.

6 Sadiyah Geyer

At the core of their endeavour lies the use of cutting-edge tools and methodologies, notably the concept of "point clouds." These 3D representations, born from laser scans and photogrammetry, unlock a wealth of information hidden within the intricacies of heritage structures. Armed with an investigative spirit, these students set out to unveil the mysteries surrounding their chosen historic sites. This narrative unfolds as they navigate digital terrain models, elevation models, surface models, and contour line models. These advanced technologies augment their ability to scrutinise, dissect, and comprehend their designated historical locations in unprecedented detail. Through these tools, they transcend temporal constraints, unveiling hidden narratives etched into the architectural marvels.

Yet, the journey is far from simple, marked by challenges, imperfections, and occasional data gaps within the complex point clouds. This story does not shy away from acknowledging these limitations. Instead, it emphasises their importance as catalysts for growth and refinement. The students demonstrate a commitment to critical analysis and adaptability, embracing a spirit of continuous improvement fuelled by their unending curiosity. The narrative unfolds across diverse historic sites, each presenting unique complexities. One such site is the Lady Bird Johnson Wildflower Center, a testament to the natural beauty of Texas. Their central focus is the Wildflower Center's central tower, adorned with organic stone and brickwork. Capturing its unique design and texture proves challenging.

To overcome these hurdles, students delve into ground control point systems, meticulously positioning control points at various elevations for accuracy. Colour, texture, and proximity to the tower become guiding principles. The narrative chronicles their journey, transitioning from raw point clouds to high-resolution 3D textured meshes, breathing life into the structure. Throughout their expedition, students master animation, weaving progression from drafts to 3D textured meshes. Vignettes allow the exploration of angles beyond physical constraints. The narrative offers glimpses into interior scans, stone wall textures, and hidden chambers, showcasing technology's power in unravelling the past.

From the towering arches to the subterranean chambers of the Seaholm Intake Building, the journey continues. This site presents challenges, with machinery obstructions obscuring discovery. In this labyrinthine environment, students employ Unmanned Aerial Vehicles (UAVs) and multiple camera angles, culminating in pristine 3D textured meshes that reveal the building's secrets. The narrative unveils the intricate process of merging 3D laser scans, photogrammetry, and image capture to construct digital representations. Students uncover subterranean chambers and hidden structures with meticulous detail, shedding light on historical functions and mysteries within the Seaholm Intake Building.

This journey exemplifies the synergy between technology and heritage, a testament to the enduring quest to unearth untold stories of the past. In the chapter, readers delve deeper into the intricacies of this remarkable voyage, witnessing firsthand the fusion of technology and tradition that revitalises the study of historic architecture. Through the lens of dedicated students, the past is reimagined, and the future of historical exploration takes on a vibrant, dynamic form.

Finally, in Chapter 5, Observing/Performing the (Pandemic) Every Day: Photographic Writing as a Curating Tool in Online Architectural Education, Bilge Beril Kapusuz Balci explores how the intricate relationship between photography and architecture has a rich history, intertwining facets of communication, documentation, critical reinterpretation of the built environment, and educational contexts. Within architectural education, photography has traditionally served as a passive medium, offering students glimpses of architectural wonders through lecture slides, books, and journals. However, the educational landscape is evolving, encouraging students to become 'active observers' who harness photography as a pedagogical tool, transforming how they perceive and interact with the built world.

Recently, the COVID-19 pandemic, coupled with the proliferation of architectural imagery on social media, has added layers of complexity to this relationship. In response, this chapter delves into the pedagogical strategies and outcomes of the course "Image Construction and Architectural Photography" taught online at Gazi University's Faculty of Architecture during the pandemic. This innovative course challenges conventional boundaries, extending its scope into urban studies and visual culture, all viewed through an ethnographic lens, with photography as the primary tool. The course's overarching goal is to redefine architectural photography, breaking free from its static representation role. Drawing inspiration from scholars like Bruno Latour and Albena Yaneva, it encourages students to explore 'the everyday' through photographic narratives of architectural spaces. This approach equips students with a critical and performative tool, enabling them to communicate about architecture using a visual language.

One of the course's transformative exercises had students observe and capture their pandemic-altered daily lives and urban surroundings for 30 days. This task fostered a deeper connection between students and their environments, turning their routines into active explorations. Photography became the bridge between observation and critical engagement, allowing students to research the complex dimensions at play in the built environment. This chapter argues that photographic writing serves as both a "curating" tool and a means of personal and societal healing within online architectural education. It empowers students to curate their experiences and simultaneously cure their constrained daily lives. Beyond the pandemic, this pedagogical approach constructs a framework highlighting the symbiotic relationship between photography and everyday life, emphasising the transformative and healing potential of the ordinary.

Photography, as employed in this course, disrupted students' routines and transformed their perceptions of their immediate surroundings. It nurtured a critical perspective, enabling students to better decipher the multifaceted aspects and agencies within the built environment. This approach extends beyond pandemic conditions, offering promise in architectural education by harnessing photography's agency for visual research and storytelling.

In conclusion, this chapter underscores photography's pivotal role in reshaping architectural education in the digital age and during crises like the COVID-19 pandemic. It advocates for an approach that transforms students into active participants in architectural discourse, empowering them not only to observe but also to critically engage with the built environment. Through innovative pedagogy and the power of photography, students can gain a profound understanding of architecture and its intricate relationship with everyday life.

In summary then, the authors of this book come together to offer unique and varied insights into contemporary discourses on technology and teaching architecture and interior architecture in the age of digital design and COVID-19. They showcase unique ways in which educators are now using technology in architectural and design teaching, whether that be new technologies applied as a direct result of COVID-19 or pre-existing ones now operative in the post-COVID context, and, in doing so, they underline how technology in design teaching is now being used as a tool to aid, reshape, deconstruct, and challenge the educational methods in architecture-related fields.

1 The Augmented Studio

Teaching and Learning in Digital Space

Rebecca Disney, Naomi House, and Francesca Murialdo

Introduction

As a physical and pedagogical entity, the Design Studio embraces and fosters collaboration beyond its physical borders; however, the move to online teaching and learning during the COVID-19 pandemic in 2020 presented significant challenges to the delivery of architecture and design education, especially in terms of transposing the 'studio' environment – its 'signature pedagogy' – to a virtual alternative. Prompting a deep reflection on and rethinking of teaching and learning within this context, it is our contention that this experience deserves a new empirical framework able to challenge existing pedagogic practices that are fundamentally resistant to change.[1]

Reviewing a year in the life of the BA (Hons) Interior Architecture programme at Middlesex University in London, we explore how the use of digital platforms signalled an emergent spatial typology, investigating pedagogical engagement in a digitally connected learning environment, that sits within the broader context of the Internet of Things (IoT) – networked physical objects and devices – and more latterly, the Internet of Spaces (IoS) – an expansion of the IoT that encompasses the built environment. Further, since the pandemic, new forms of artificial intelligence (AI) have begun to significantly impact upon this learning environment, once again challenging the efficacy of the Design Studio as a pedagogic space. Articulating a future scenario where the Design Studio will necessarily exist as a mixed reality entity, we propose the 'Augmented Studio', superimposing existing and emerging digital technologies over the physical studio environment to construct a new pedagogic landscape within which we prepare, shape, and equip teaching and learning moving forward. What precedents exist for this augmented environment? How might these inform the evolution of a new pedagogic framework for spatial design education, and how might future pedagogy continue to be shaped by digital-era technologies?

Scenario

The onset of lockdown in the UK in March 2020 precipitated a global shift in how we teach and learn, simultaneously closing down physical spaces to open up new – or at least largely untested – digital environments, within which the everyday 'business'[2] of the University would now be conducted. For courses delivered primarily through conventional modes of teaching, this shift from the physical to the virtual was affected with little disruption to the academic calendar, and delivery methods largely mirrored existing ones.

However, for practice-based programmes such as those within schools of Art and Design, the move to a virtual studio demanded the reformulation of both content and pedagogic approach, focusing attention on student engagement both in terms of their (and our own) intellectual and emotional resilience within an entirely virtual learning environment (VLE) and challenging us to consider how this unfamiliar teaching and learning space might foster innovative pedagogic strategies.

As such, the 'Expanded Studio' that we developed during the pandemic became an adaptive solution to teaching and learning as well as a new space of pedagogic resistance that continues to inform and reshape how we teach and learn in a post-pandemic, educational landscape.

'Push Button' Education

The defining role of technology in education is not a new frontier. Since the end of the Second World War, technology has played a central role in shaping education. During this period, enthusiasm for technology as a tool was able to provide infinite new resources and solutions, which produced a number of theories and methods for new learning pedagogies based on automation.

Simon Ramo, who developed the intercontinental ballistic missile, envisioned the future of education as completely rooted in an interactive, computer-based, automatically adaptable learning methodology. His technologically sophisticated approach was tailored around individual students, whose interactions and academic progress were to be continually monitored.[3] The role of the instructor was also contested in Ramo's educational model, where machines delivered content and the teacher acted as mentor and/or supervisor. What remained more or less static was the physical teaching, learning location, and the scheduling. Within this techno-pedagogy, students still attended courses in a physical space equipped with the necessary technologies to deliver content, and they were all learning at the same time.

Another precedent prompted by the technological revolution underway during this period was the Open University – a project founded by the Labour Government in the UK, under Harold Wilson in 1969, with the aim of widening access to higher education, promoting equality of opportunity and social mobility. The Open University began enrolling students in 1971 and was initially based at Alexandra Palace in North London, using the television studios, and editing facilities which had been vacated by the British Broadcasting Corporation (BBC), to broadcast its courses. It was designed to enable students to study off-campus, anywhere in the world, challenging the notion of a rooted and static space of and for education.

However, these 'push-button' models for educating the masses are not the only relevant precedents here. In May 1966, architect Cedric Price published his proposal for updating architectural education in the Architect's Journal –*The National School Plan*.[4] Price believed that education was constrained by the differing agendas of architectural schools across the country. In his vision, a mobile student population would access shared courses through videos, transcripts, or live events, enabling flexibility (in practical and methodological terms) and providing 'advantages to be gained from mass participation'.[5] An enthusiasm for technology was key to his design philosophy, and the tools he imagined were intended as a means by which to democratise architectural education throughout the UK.

A few decades later, the advent of the internet once again transformed the relationship between education and technology – everyone everywhere (in theory) would now be able to access an infinite amount of knowledge through the World Wide Web. Indeed, some of the most radical and revolutionary educational formats rely on the availability of the internet to guarantee open access to education for many. An example is the MOOC or Massive Open Online Course, which is free to anyone with internet access and has gained popularity in recent years due to its ability to provide education to individuals who may not have access to traditional educational institutions.[6] However, MOOCs are overtly egalitarian pedagogic spaces, but they nevertheless assume equality of access to the internet itself rather than find ways to navigate the factors that impede access, such as geographical region and cost.[7]

Digital Dialectics[8]

One lens through which to contemplate and analyse our recent experience of adopting digital platforms in order to facilitate a shift to online teaching during the pandemic is digital anthropology. [8, 9] First defined by Daniel Miller and Heather Horst in 2012 as a 'subdivision of the discipline of Anthropology, that has emerged in response to developments in digital infrastructure and technology that have increasingly become intrinsically embedded within most daily lives',[10] digital anthropology examines the intersection of digital technologies and social and cultural practices.

As technology continues to evolve and permeate all aspects of our lives, including education, it is essential to consider its impact through a sociocultural lens. With the advent of new technologies, such as augmented and virtual reality (VR), gamification, and artificial intelligence, the future of education is being reshaped in unprecedented ways. Digital anthropology seeks to understand these changes, including how they affect the teaching and learning process, classroom dynamics, and the role of educators in this new digital landscape. By examining the impact of these new technologies on educational practices and student experiences, digital anthropology can provide valuable insights into how we can use them to create more engaging, effective, and inclusive learning environments.

The global COVID-19 pandemic established a new norm in which digital technologies became integrated into our everyday routines and activities, transforming the way we communicate and interact with each other. The rapid shift to remote work and online communication necessitated the adoption of new tools and terminologies, as we became increasingly reliant on digital platforms and virtual environments to maintain and manage our social connectivity. Inhabiting digital territories, we now share screens and virtual spaces to overcome physical distance and enable remote presence. This shift has led us to make conscious decisions about how to present ourselves in the digital realm, such as the choice to blur our domestic background or reveal personal details that imply intimacy and confidence.

Many academics who transitioned to online studios reported feeling 'scattered by the pandemic; made distant, yet not remote. In the Zoom grid, we found ourselves sitting next to each other, in new ways, different for each meeting'[11] – what Jane Rendell refers to as 'experimental spaces of pedagogical process'.[12] Our working patterns, time zones, and subsequent behaviours were seamlessly modified. Daniel Miller and Jolynna Sinanan argue that latent qualities of humanness are revealed/drawn out/uncovered/evolved as new digital artefacts and platforms are created,[13] and recent psychological research evidences that 'experiences while in the virtual world, also modify attitudes and behaviours in the physical world as well'.[14]

The COVID-19 pandemic spurred a rapid and extensive adoption of digital technologies, resulting in significant transformations in information creation and sharing as well as in the dynamics of individual and team interactions. These changes are anticipated to have enduring implications, with digital and virtual environments projected to persist beyond the shift from remote back to in-person work.

It has become commonplace to witness 3D digital scanning technology being used to examine hidden archaeological sites on mainstream television[15] or VR to offer architectural and decorative permutations of viewers' homes.[16] The digital is now instantly accessible, providing alternative spaces that users can inhabit as themselves or within an alternative identity. Interior spaces are increasingly permeable and open to new modes of occupation, as Joshua M. Bluteau describes, 'this gap between the online and offline worlds becomes so close that the two bleed into one another until they are enmeshed, immersive cohabitation'.[17]

The Metaverse: From the Internet to the Internet of Spaces

The term 'Metaverse' – a combination of the prefix 'meta-' and the word 'universe', 'meta' derived from the Greek word 'meta', which means 'beyond' or 'transcending', and 'universe' that means the totality of all physical and metaphysical existence – refers to a hypothetical future state of the internet, in which users can seamlessly move between physical and virtual spaces and engage in a wide range of activities.

Neal Stephenson's novel *Snow Crash*, which was published in 1992, is widely credited as the first use of the term 'Metaverse'. In the novel, Stephenson describes a virtual world called the Metaverse, which is a fully immersive and interactive VR space where users can communicate with each other and with digital objects in real time and engage in various activities such as gaming, socialising, and commerce. Users in the Metaverse can create their own virtual identities, or 'avatars', with which to mediate these interactions. This virtual world is not limited to just one platform or technology but instead is a complex ecosystem of interconnected virtual environments, devices, and systems.

The Metaverse is currently referred to today as an integration of several emerging technologies, such as blockchain, augmented reality (AR), VR, and AI, with the aim of creating a cohesive vision. The Metaverse is not intended to replace physical experiences; rather, it seeks to enhance them by providing new and innovative opportunities for global interaction. The Metaverse is a virtual space that can be accessed from anywhere, offering unique features such as global connectivity, infinite scalability, and flexible customisation options. These features make it possible to experience things that are otherwise impossible or difficult to achieve in the physical world.

To understand the Metaverse better, it is useful to look at the evolution of the internet as a global system that is continually in flux. In the 1990s, when the internet emerged, it largely operated as a repository of data – a world of infinite and easily accessible knowledge. In the 2000s, the internet evolved into a social space enabling the connectivity of people via platforms such as Myspace (formally MySpace), Facebook, and Twitter, and in 2007, with the launch of the first Apple iPhone, the internet became, in effect, an extension of the human body. Although the term was first coined in 1999 by Kevin Ashton, executive director of the Auto-ID Center, it was in 2010 that the IoT – a network of physical objects and devices that utilise digital networks to independently share information and data – was acknowledged as a global concept, with China signalling its intention to invest heavily in the IoT as an industry.[18]

With the onset of the global pandemic, we support the notion that a new version of the internet has come into being through the necessary utilisation of digital platforms to initially replicate face-to-face encounters. We refer to this iteration as the IoS, which connects physical and virtual spaces by leveraging a combination of technologies to enable the creation of a fully interconnected ecosystem of physical and digital environments, allowing users to seamlessly move between the two.

One way that the IoS can connect physical and virtual spaces is through the use of sensors and IoT devices. These devices will be embedded in physical spaces such as buildings, cities, and transportation systems and will collect data in real time. This data can be sent to the cloud, where it will be analysed using AI and machine learning algorithms to gain insights into how people are using and interacting with and within these spaces. This information can then be used to optimise the design of these spaces and enhance the user experience – one such approach that has been gaining traction in recent years is the concept of a 'digital twin'.[19]

The integration of AR/VR technologies into the IoS is expected to enhance the way users interact with physical spaces in the future. By overlaying digital information onto physical spaces, AR/VR technologies create an immersive and interactive experience that blurs the line between the physical and virtual worlds. For instance, AR technology can be used to overlay information such as directions, product information, or historical context onto real-world objects, making the physical space literally 'augmented'.

The Expanded Studio

Re-arranging the Furniture

Interior Architecture at Middlesex University is concerned with the study of interiors that adapt and remodel buildings and spaces through architectural

Figure 1.1 Interior Architecture at Middlesex University.

intervention, respecting and connecting with existing site contexts for long-term use. Projects focus on the relationship between the new design and the existing building.

However, teaching and learning in design education is not a linear process – every day, we enter the studio and begin by (re)arranging the furniture to accommodate planned activities – Design Studio teaching is largely reactive, responding in real time to conversations in a tutorial or around outcomes of a workshop.

Working across different media simultaneously, we pin up drawings and references, sketch over design proposals, cut and glue models, view case studies online, and discuss ideas in groups. On campus, we move between the studio, the library, the materials room, and the workshop. But we also meet off-campus to visit project sites, exhibitions, and exemplar buildings and interiors. Design Studios are, as educator and architect, Thomas A. Dutton states, 'active sites where students are engaged intellectually and socially, shifting between analytic, synthetic, and evaluative modes of thinking in different sets of activities'.[20]

But how do you 'rearrange the furniture' in a digital teaching and learning environment, and how do we work collectively and collaboratively in this space? Moving to a digital studio in March 2020, we had to reformulate both content and pedagogical approach – the set-up of this digital teaching and learning space involved a deep reflection on what we value within our existing educational models and what we might teach and learn moving forward.

Drawing upon the work of Donald Schön in *The Reflective Practitioner* (1987), architect and educator James Benedict Brown extrapolates that the Design Studio is simultaneously 'the site of a conflict between the traditions of the discipline and the economic pressures of the contemporary university', 'a period of time in the teaching calendar', 'a large field of both teaching method and pedagogies', and a 'culture'.[21]

One challenge for the online classroom is, as James Benedict Brown states, 'resolutely not how can we recreate the architecture studio online. It is how we can liberate our discipline from the assumption that an ill-defined space, time, pedagogy, and culture is the only way to teach design. It is an opportunity to re-construct architecture education in a more critical, inclusive, and democratic way'.[22]

The 'Expanded Studio' we designed merged the physical and theoretical structures from both the real and the digital worlds. The ambition was to retain 'in real-life' pedagogy, adding the benefits of being part of a digitally networked space. We also had to investigate the characteristics of this new environment to make sure we were not proposing a mere transition from a physical to a digital studio, exploring how this transition could happen in practical terms, by offering a range of choices and specialist spaces, and supporting multiple channels of communication that were continuously open. These channels needed to enable 1:1, 1: many, and many: many exchanges as well as a degree of flexibility to allow students to move seamlessly between these

16 *Rebecca Disney, Naomi House, and Francesca Murialdo*

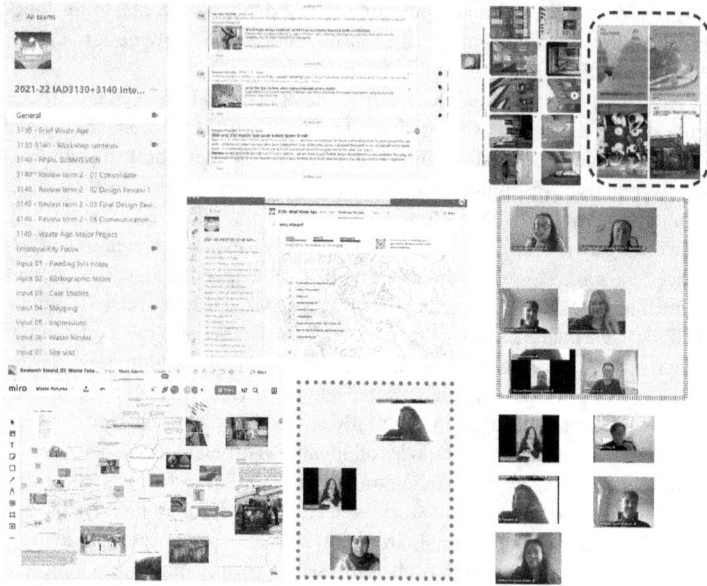

Figure 1.2 The Expanded Studio/Interaction and Interaction.

digital spaces, much like they would have done on campus, ranging across rooms and buildings. Remapping the structure of our teaching and learning, aligning each activity with a specific 'space', and equipping these 'environments' with particular features, according to our shared lexicon, each 'room' was allocated a virtual pin-up board, a few 'meeting tables', tutorial spaces, an archive, and several integrated digital tools.

Figure 1.3 The Expanded Studio – The Modelmaking Workshops.

The 'Expanded Studio' was a space that adapted to our needs, enabling us to run simultaneous activities. For example, we had students connecting with the Digital Workshop at the University, which was managed on-site by workshop technicians, through a 'Digital Pathway room' that had been set up to store examples, samples, tutorials, and experiments, alongside being used to actually produce 'real' laser-cut and 3D-printed models from a student studying from Japan.

Time and Timetabling

During the pandemic, time developed elastic properties; some activities were slower and more cumbersome online, but also time that was usually dedicated to teaching and learning was overlaid, and sometimes conflated, with domestic routines, home schooling, caring responsibilities, whilst adapting also to different time zones.

The 'Expanded Studio', with its synchronous and asynchronous teaching and learning model, enabled students to become more independent from the programme, using live tutorials as an anchor point in the day, attending in real time, and/or reviewing inputs at a later point and with the advantage of slowing down, repeating, or skipping components of the delivery. In this context, building interaction and engagement was one of the main aims. The disruption of the relational aspect of teaching and learning, and the immobility and the un-natural behaviours prompted by the software, such as interpreting conversation cues and the distraction of both hearing and seeing oneself whilst communicating with others, impacted in both predictable and unpredictable ways on students, in particular challenging the conventions of peer-to-peer learning and the collaborative aspects of our pedagogic practice. A shared

Figure 1.4 The Expanded Studio – The Global Classroom.

repository where students could browse through everybody else's work and listen into tutorials or reviews (live or recorded) received positive feedback – anecdotally, students said they engaged more fully than they would traditionally have done by listening to live reviews.

We also selected software that is able to support collaboration and group work – to brainstorm, edit, curate, and share ideas and projects. Some workshops, such as those for the Writing Portfolio (our version of the dissertation), really benefitted from being staged online, and students seemed more focused and productive. The flexibility of spaces and time also made it possible to deliver a very successful 'vertical studio' with common activities and resources across different year groups – something more difficult to achieve in the Design Studio due to timetabling constraints.

Whilst the activity of teaching and learning during the pandemic shifted to the 'Expanded Studio', the outcomes produced by students working in this space also become more attuned to the digital landscape. Although our students already worked in digital space, researching, designing, and communicating their design projects using an array of platforms and software, the sudden move to the digital learning environment prompted a greater focus on video and audio outcomes. A publication that showcases graduating students' works – Draft magazine – has since the summer of 2020 been reshaped to reflect the needs and requirements of a digital journal, integrating with existing digital platforms and social media.

The Augmented Studio: Manifesto for a Future Pedagogy?

In April 2020, Caroline Levander and Peter Decherney questioned if online teaching is 'education's holy grail, equalising opportunity and access, opening up classrooms to the masses, and now ensuring that the world can continue to be educated while a pandemic closes public spaces, including schools and universities?'[23] Although we should not assume that online learning environments are unproblematic in terms of audience accessibility – as architect and educator Harriet Harriss has identified, 'These platforms may allocate each user equal inches of screen space, but simultaneously surrender a window into our otherwise private domestic interiors, revealing often staggering economic differentials between students ...'[24] – we can nevertheless embrace the vision that online learning environments might in some way engender more open and collaborative spaces for learning.[25]

In a post-lockdown scenario, teaching and learning within our programme has in some ways seen a return to the signature pedagogies of our discipline – the Design Studio itself has been reinstated as the space within which most of the teaching and learning occurs. The 'Expanded Studio' that we established now sits alongside the physical space of the Design Studio, augmenting it with access to adjacent online classrooms that enable students to attend 'live' teaching events whilst working from home in COVID quarantine, for example. More recent global events, such as the War in Ukraine, prompted some of our students to return home in response to family crisis without being forced to miss significant presentations or tutorial discussions. This ability to stay connected has also meant that students, as well as staff, have been able to remain in touch even when a common cold, for example, prevents face-to-face contact.

Middlesex University is based in London, and this design context has always supported our programme with exhibitions, conferences, and 'live' case studies available on the doorstep. Our 'Expanded Studio' benefits from an open teaching team: former students, graduate academic assistants, practitioners, and colleagues from other programmes and universities are integral to this, contributing and supporting the programme with talks, workshops, and reviews.

With lockdown, what initially seemed to limit teaching and learning instead offered a range of new opportunities, consolidating old and enabling new long-term collaborations with partner institutions and scholars around the globe, thereby augmenting our existing networks. Although we were unable to access the public spaces of our city over this period, entire archives and collections became (and remain) digitally open and easily accessible to all. A dense programme of relevant talks and symposia during this time also helped demonstrate the potential of digital media to reach speakers and audiences across the globe, including those who might previously have been excluded from participating, not to mention the environmental benefits of this digital nomadism.

Beyond the blended learning that the 'Augmented Studio' offers, however, is a more significant shift in how we archive our programme. The capacity to house an entire course within the cloud, updating content as we need to without erasing previous content as and when the University's VLE might require it, also gives us the agency to evolve our programme as an iterative entity.

Fundamentally, the 'Augmented Studio' is an environment that activates teaching and learning across borders, breaking down hierarchies and opening up dialogue with individuals and organisations outside the Academy. Continuous and infinitely expandable, the 'Augmented Studio' enables students to develop their own trajectory of interests, extending beyond the territory of the traditional Design Studio into the digital realm, where all interactions take place outside the conventional confines of space and time. Although the assimilation of the physical and digital Design Studio has highlighted its resistance to pedagogic change, it has nevertheless provided the opportunity to engender a new space for teaching and learning that is at once familiar and yet also strange. And this dialectic between the real and the virtual is continuously filtered by the overlapping environments that we simultaneously inhabit.

By 'breaking free' of the physical boundaries of learning and expanding the Design Studio into the multiverse of digital environments through the action of augmentation, we must harness the power of technology to challenge traditional teaching and learning methods. 'In short, online learning opens up the possibility of teacher-student-machine symbiosis and a way of augmenting, rather than replacing, human pedagogy'.[26]

'The Augmented Studio – A Manifesto' aims to demonstrate how the widespread availability of new technologies can be leveraged to enhance pedagogical practices in the future. The manifesto highlights several opportunities for future learning spaces enabled by these technologies.

Firstly, it advocates for a Safe Space where students can feel empowered to take risks and experiment freely. This would be facilitated using supportive digital tools that encourage exploration and experimentation. Gamification – the process of applying game design elements and mechanics to non-game contexts – has emerged as an experimental tool that can enhance student engagement, motivation, and learning outcomes, fostering experimentation by encouraging learners to take risks, foster collaboration, and participate in teamwork.

Secondly, the manifesto calls for an Open Space that allows for a seamless integration of digital tools and resources into the learning process. This would enable learners to engage with a diverse range of multimedia content in a fluid and flexible manner.

Thirdly, an Inclusive Space is advocated, one that is more democratic and accessible, challenges hierarchies, and breaks down barriers of gender, ethnicity, class, and geographical limitations. This would be facilitated by the use of technologies that enable remote learning and collaboration, allowing for a more diverse and global student body.

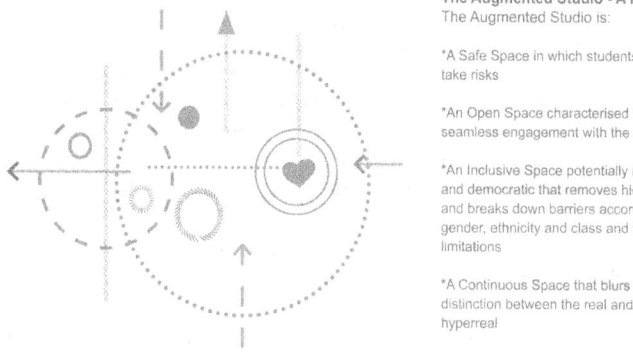

Figure 1.5 The Augmented Studio – A Manifesto.

Finally, the manifesto envisions a Continuous Space that blurs the distinction between the real and the hyperreal. This would enable learners to engage with immersive and interactive digital environments that enhance their understanding of real-world phenomena and promote deeper learning.

'The Augmented Studio – A Manifesto' represents an important call to action for educators and institutions to embrace the potential of new technologies to create dynamic and transformative learning environments that are better suited to the needs of modern learners.

Afterword

This chapter offers a reflective account of teaching and learning during the pandemic and addresses the rapidly shifting pedagogical landscape that underpins the post-COVID Augmented Design Studio. Through the lens of digital anthropology, this landscape collides the material and immaterial worlds. Our digital experiences, although conducted in the infinite realm of the internet, are nevertheless enacted in 'real' places and shaped by our surrounding environment – our synchronous and asynchronous interactions in digital space represent simultaneous phenomenological encounters between our bodies and the Metaverse within which they coexist.

L. Osler and J. Krueger characterise these phenomenological encounters through Japanese philosopher Tetsuro Watsuji's[27] concept of *aidagara* or betweenness – in particular 'subjective spatiality' – which they argue offers 'a prescient analysis anticipating modern technologically-mediated forms of expression, connection, and engagement'.[28] Further, they suggest, 'The "dialectical" character of betweenness indicates that it is not something fixed or found pre-given in the world; nor is betweenness simply an a priori category of experience. Rather, it is a mode of being-in-relation-to-others that is actively *constructed*'.[29] As such, the Augmented Studio frames both the actions and interactions of the user within the context of an IoS, establishing and facilitating a community of learning that is contingent upon understanding what it means to be human.

Notes

1 James Benedict Brown, "From denial to acceptance: a turning point for design studio in architecture education," Distance Design Education (2020), https://distancedesigneducation.com/2020/05/11/from-denial-to-acceptance-a-turning-point-for-design-studio-in-architecture-education/, accessed May 12, 2022.
2 Sharon Mistretta describes how, 'The education community scrambled to enact video-based platforms such as Zoom, Microsoft Teams, and Google Meet to retrofit the classroom into a business-meeting paradigm for students and teachers sequestered at home.' Mistretta, Sharon, "The Metaverse—An Alternative Education Space," AI, Computer Science and Robotics Technology (2022): 1–23.
3 Simon Ramo, "A New Technique of Education," Engineering and Science Monthly XXI (October 1957): 17–22, http://calteches.library.caltech.edu/1767/1/ramo.pdf, accessed May 12, 2022.

4 "National School Plan," Cedric Price Collection,1966, https://archiveshub.jisc.ac.uk/search/archives/8a4edd68-4f7b-3319-9480-d1a9d62cc943, accessed May 10, 2022.
5 Zenon Bankowski, Maksymilian Del Mar and Paul Maharg, *The Arts and the Legal Academy: Beyond Text in Legal Education* (Abingdon: Routledge, 2013), p. 43.
6 MOOCs are offered by a variety of universities and organisations and cover a wide range of topics. https://www.mooc.org/
7 Ani Petrosyan, 'As of January 2023, there were 5.16 billion internet users worldwide, which is 64.4 percent of the global population. Of this total, 4.76 billion, or 59.4 percent of the world's population, were social media users'. Ani Petrosyan, "Internet and Social Media Users in the World 2023." Statista. February 14, 2023. https://www.statista.com/statistics/617136/digital-population-worldwide/#:~:text=As%20of%20January%202023%2C%20there.https://www.statista.com/statistics/617136/digital-population-worldwide/#:~:text=As%20of%20January%202023%2C%20there,population%2C%20were%20social%20media%20users, accessed April 17, 2023.
8 For Daniel Miller and Heather Horst, digital anthropology is 'dialectical', Daniel Miller and Heather A. Horst, "Six principles for a digital anthropology", in *Digital Anthropology*, eds. Haidy Geismar and Hannah Knox (Abingdon: Routledge, 2021), p. 22.
9 According to Daniel Miller, anthropology is 'the discipline most likely to situate new technologies within a much wider cultural and social context and thereby appreciate the inherent contradictions and complexities that emerge from the larger study of their use and consequence'. Daniel Miller, "Digital Anthropology." Cambridge Encyclopedia of Anthropology. July 17, 2019, https://www.anthroencyclopedia.com/entry/digital-anthropology, accessed May 12, 2022.
10 Tom Boellstorff, "Rethinking digital anthropology", in Digital Anthropology, eds. Daniel Miller and Heather A. Horst (London: Routledge, 2020), p. 39–60.
11 Jane Rendell, "Seven Studies for 'A Holding'" (23 March – 31 May 2020), in *Remote Practices: Architecture at a Distance* (London: Lund Humphries, 2022), 95.
12 Ibid.
13 Daniel Miller and Jolynna Sinanan posit a 'theory of attainment' discussing latent qualities of humanness, Daniel Miller and Joynna Sinanan. *Webcam* (Cambridge: Polity Press, 2014),1–23.
14 David Markowitz and Jeremy Bailenson, Virtual Reality and Communication. Last modified: February 27, 2019. DOI: 10.1093/OBO/9780199756841-0222.
15 *Italy's Invisible cities*, https://www.bbc.co.uk/programmes/b088nl33
16 *Your Home Made Perfect*, https://www.bbc.co.uk/programmes/m00048xf
17 Joshua M. Bluteau, "Legitimising Digital Anthropology through Immersive Cohabitation. Becoming an Observing Participant in a Blended Digital Landscape". *Ethnography* 22, no. 2 (2021): 267–285.
18 UNSEF, "A Brief History of the IoT", Workshop on Internet of Things Development for the Promotion of Information Economy, Boracay, Philippines, May 14, 2015.
19 A digital twin is a virtual replica of a physical object, process, or system (for example a building). It is created by using real-time data from sensors and other sources to create a digital model that mirrors the physical object or system.
20 Tugce Ecem Tufek, citing Dutton 1987, "An Unexpected Shift to an Online Design Studio Course: Student Insights on Design critiques," *International Journal of Art & Design Education* 41, no. 1 (2022): 158–159. DOI: 10.1111/jade.12400, https://onlinelibrary.wiley.com/doi/epdf/10.1111/jade.12400, accessed May 12, 2022.
21 Benedict Brown, accessed May 12, 2022.
22 Ibid.

23 Peter Decherney and Caroline Levander, "Can Remote Teaching Make Us More Human?" *Inside Higher Ed* (2020), https://www.insidehighered.com/digital-learning/blogs/education-time-corona/can-remote-teaching-make-us-more-human, accessed May 12, 2022.
24 Harriet Harriss cited in Benedict Brown, accessed May 12, 2022.
25 Leo Sands, 'but other students found the move to remote education had made learning easier, with disabled students benefiting in particular', "University student complaints over courses hit record" BBC News, May 4, 2022, https://www.bbc.co.uk/news/uk-61314662.amp, accessed May 12, 2022.
26 Liz W. Faber, "Augmenting Human Pedagogy: A Cultural History of Automation in Teaching," *Popular Culture Studies Journal* 9, no. 1 (2021): 59.
27 Tetsuro Watsuji was a Japanese historian and moral philosopher, 1889–1960, and part of the Kyoto School. His concept of aidagara is a set of phenomenological ideas that predate the publication of Merleau-Ponty's, *The Phenomenology of Perception*, first published in 1945.
28 Lucy Osler and Joel Krueger, "Taking Watsuji Online: Betweenness and Expression in Online Spaces", *Continental Philosophy Review* 55 (2022): 77–99, https://doi.org/10.1007/s11007-021-09548-7, accessed April 14, 2023.
29 Ibid.

Bibliography

Patricia Arcilla, "New York to Complete First Prefabricated "Micro-Apartments" this Year." *ArchDaily*. February 24, 2015. Accessed February 26, 2015, http://www.archdaily.com/?p=602157

Zenon Bankowski, Maksymilian Del Mar and Paul Maharg, *The Arts and the Legal Academy: Beyond Text in Legal Education* (Abingdon: Routledge, 2013).

James Benedict Brown, 'From denial to acceptance: a turning point for design studio in architecture education', Originally published on the Distance Design Education blog, supported by the Design Research Society Pedagogy SIG and The Open University (UK) Design Group. 2020, https://distancedesigneducation.com/2020/05/11/from-denial-to-acceptance-aturning-point-for-design-studio-in-architecture-education/

Joshua M. Bluteau, "Legitimising Digital Anthropology through Immersive Cohabitation. Becoming an Observing Participant in a Blended Digital Landscape." *Ethnography* 22 no. 2 (2021): 267–285.

Barry Curtis, Naomi House and Monika Parrinder, "Towards seamful living", in *Interior Futures*, eds. Grame Brooker, Harriet Harriss and Kevin Walker (Yountville, California: Crucible Press, 2019).

Peter Decherney and Caroline Levander, "Can Remote Teaching Make Us More Human?" *Inside Higher Ed*. April 22, 2020, https://www.insidehighered.com/digital-learning/blogs/education-time-corona/can-remote-teaching-make-us-more-human

Mark Dorrian, 'Pan Scroll Zoom 20:10 PM in inner Mongolia', *Drawing Matter*. 2021, https://drawingmatter.org/10pm-in-inner-mongolia/

Liz W. Faber, "Augmenting Human Pedagogy: A Cultural History of Automation in Teaching." *Popular Culture Studies Journal* 9 no. 1 (2021): 44.

Aminreza Iranmanesh and Zeynep Onur, "Mandatory Virtual Design Studio for All: Exploring the Transformations of Architectural Education amidst the Global Pandemic." *The International Journal of Art and Design Education* 14, no. 1 (2021): 251–267. https://onlinelibrary.wiley.com/doi/10.1111/jade.12350

Patience Lamunu Opiyo Lueth, "The architectural design studio as a learning environment: a qualitative exploration of architecture design student learning experiences in design studios from first- through fourth-year." (2008). *Retrospective Theses and Dissertations*. 15788, https://www.proquest.com/openview/944c2ccabba92ca22852 8a06a947d3c7/1?pq-origsite=gscholar&cbl=18750

Daniel Miller and Heather Horst, "Digital Anthropology", *The Cambridge Encyclopaedia of Anthropology*, https://www.anthroencyclopedia.com/entry/digital-anthropology

Daniel Miller and Heather Horst, "Six principles for a digital anthropology", in *Digital Anthropology*, eds. Haidy Geismar and Hannah Knox (Abingdon: Routledge, 2021).

Daniel Miller and Jolynna Sinanan, *Webcam* (Cambridge: Polity Press, 2014).

Sharon Mistretta, "The Metaverse—An Alternative Education Space." *AI, Computer Science and Robotics Technology* (2022): 1–23.

Lucy Osler and Joel Krueger, "Taking Watsuji Online: Betweenness and Expression in Online Spaces." *Continental Philosophy Review* 55 (2022): 77–99. https://doi.org/10.1007/s11007-021-09548-7

Ani Petrosyan, "Internet and Social Media Users in the World 2023." Statista. February 14, 2023, https://www.statista.com/statistics/617136/digital-population-worldwide/#:~:text=As%20of%20January%202023%2C%20there.https://www.statista.com/statistics/617136/digital-population-worldwide/#:~:text=As%20of%20January%202023%2C%20there,population%2C%20were%20social%20media%20users

Cedric Price, 'National School Plan', *Architects' Journal*, May 25, 1966, https://cedricprice.anticipatorydesign.info/2020/04/06/national-school-plan-2/

Simon Ramo, "Method and apparatus for interactive, computer-based, automatically adaptable learning." 2013. U.S. Patent 8,606,170 issued December 10, 2013. https://patentimages.storage.googleapis.com/3b/96/2d/b18e4996c3302b/US8606170.pdf

Jane Rendell, "Seven studies for 'A holding'" (23 March – 31 May 2020), in *Remote Practices: Architecture at a Distance* eds. Lilian Chee and Matthew Mindrup (London: Lund Humphries, 2022).

Leo Sands, "University student complaints over courses hit record", *BBC News*, May 4, 2022, https://www.bbc.co.uk/news/uk-61314662.amp

Space Popular, 2019. https://web.archive.org/web/20230924023308/http://www.spacepopular.com/exhibitions/2019---the-venn-room

Tuğçe Ecem Tüfek, "An Unexpected Shift to an Online Design Studio Course: Student Insights on Design Critiques." *International Journal of Art & Design Education* 41 no. 1 (2022): 158–170.

UNSEF, "A Brief History of the IoT", Workshop on Internet of Things Development for the Promotion of Information Economy, Boracay, Philippines, May 14, 2015.

Tsungjuang Wang. "A New Paradigm for Design Studio Education." *The International Journal of Art and Design Education* 29, no. 2 (2010): 173–183. https://onlinelibrary.wiley.com/doi/abs/10.1111/j.1476-8070.2010.01647.x

2 Digital Twin Cities

An Instrument for Pedagogical Change

Calayde Davey

Introduction

As populations grow and urbanisation accelerates, cities face mounting pressure to develop innovative solutions to tackle the challenges confronting the built environment. Digital twin (DT) technology for cities represents a promising solution to these challenges. By enabling real-time planning and design, environmental impact assessments, community studies, or infrastructure management, digital twin cities (DTCs) can revolutionise not only how we live in urban areas but also how we work in the built environment industry as a whole.

The vision for DTCs offers exciting opportunities to revolutionise how we live and work in urban areas. The growing interest in DTCs and the increasing number of initiatives around the world illustrate the vast potential of this technology. For example, the City of Rotterdam is leveraging its urban DT to enhance various city functions. They are developing applications that provide real-time data to the fire department for emergency responses, streamline permitting processes with automated compliance checks, engage residents in co-creation for public space redesign, and explore the integration of housing company-owned DTs to collaborate on sustainability initiatives. Rotterdam aims to have a functional platform and DT by the end of 2024, promoting data-driven decision-making and urban development. As such, the successful implementation of DTCs could improve the sustainability and resilience of urban areas while enhancing the quality of life for residents.

However, the DTC future is not without its challenges. One significant obstacle is the quality of shared digital intelligence, digital skills, and data governance among people. Data-sharing among stakeholders can be complex and contentious. For instance, when developing a DT for urban infrastructure, various stakeholders like government agencies, utility companies, local communities, and private developers must collaborate to share data on underground utility networks, such as water and sewage pipes. However, each stakeholder may have proprietary data and concerns about security and privacy. Negotiating access, data standards, and usage agreements can become challenging as

DOI: 10.4324/9781003435396-3

these parties balance their interests and responsibilities, making data-sharing a complex and contentious process.

Another challenge in the digital twinning of cities is the perception that it is an exclusive and high-tech field, which can be intimidating for newcomers. This results in a shortage of people acquiring the essential digital skills necessary for the digital twinning of urban challenges. As a result, the lack of shared digital knowledge presents a significant obstacle to building and maintaining DTCs. There is also a challenge in transferring traditional and legacy knowledge between built environment practitioners and emerging intelligent digital domains of the 21st century. This lack of collective digital knowledge poses a significant obstacle to the growth and maintenance of DTCs. In essence, the need for shared digital intelligence makes digital twinning of any urban aspect challenging. Finally, ethical and social considerations must be taken into account to ensure that local DTCs are designed, deployed, and engaged with in a way that benefits all members of society and not just a privileged few.

To achieve a future where DTCs are the norm, it is imperative to foster a culture of learning and collaboration that promotes the sharing and development of digital intelligence among individuals. This is particularly critical in the built environment sector, where digital skills have become essential for future growth and development. While the COVID-19 pandemic has accelerated the adoption of digital technologies, there remains a significant gap in digital skills within the sector due to its historic reluctance to embrace innovation and new skills.[1] This situation presents a major obstacle to the advancement of 21st-century built projects and practices, which require a workforce equipped with digital competencies at all levels to drive progress forward. Therefore, it is essential to take a critical look at the gap in digital skills and expertise within the built environment domain, prioritise the development of digital competencies in education and training programs to close this gap, and prepare the built environment workforce for the demands of the future of work.

Educators play a pivotal role in addressing the digital skills gap in the built environment. In preparing learners for the future of work, there lies a new opportunity to integrate DTC development processes into core curriculum. By reframing DTCs' processes as digital training grounds rather than solely digital products, educators can not only enhance learners' digital maturity but also address the socio-economic concerns of the local community. Incorporating DTC practices into built environment education can help bridge the digital talent gap and prepare learners for the challenges that lie ahead in the digital era. This approach benefits not only learners but also contributes to the wider goal of achieving a future where DTCs are the norm.

This chapter explores the concept of DT technologies and their potential to transform the built environment industry. We highlight the importance of digital skills for the future of cities and discuss the challenges facing the industry in developing and retaining digital talent. Through the case study of the

Hatfield Digital Twin City Initiative, we have seen how a transdisciplinary approach can help to bridge the digital skills gap and prepare the next generation of professionals for the digital built environment. By taking a collaborative and holistic approach to DTC development, we can build more sustainable, efficient, and equitable cities while closing the digital skills gap. The key lessons learned and insights gained from our experiences can serve as a valuable roadmap for other cities and industries looking to embrace the digital revolution and thrive in the 21st century.

Digital Twin Cities: The Promise of a Better Urban Future

What Are Digital Twin Cities?

The emergence of data-driven digital technologies has made it possible to establish real-time feedback loops of urban systems and processes through DT technology. DTs are increasingly recognised as valuable tools to combat existing and future challenges of industry and the built environment.[2] A DT is essentially a virtual copy of a physical system or process that receives real-time data flows from the real world. A DTC is a collection of DTs of city assets and processes, which exchange data streams in real-time through a shared digital platform. A DTC consists of both *geometric* data (such as objects, buildings, roads, geographies, or environments) and *process* data (including social, manufactured, or natural systems; human or machine operational data; utility data; resource flows; or behavioural data). The goal of any DTC is to establish real-time feedback loops between urban reality, phenomena, and environments by integrating geometric and process data through a shared digital platform. The result is a digital real-time copy, or *twin*, of the city that comes *alive*.

DTCs hold great promise in addressing urban challenges. City-scale initiatives like Virtual Singapore,[3] Wellington Digital Twin City,[4] the Digital Twin Cities Centre in Sweden,[5] and national-scale initiatives in Britain and Germany are rapidly deploying digitalisation and "smart" technologies to address a wide range of urban challenges. Some DTC applications focus on complex urban interaction, such as Wellington's real-time urban mobility models[6] or Germany's land-use, energy, and extreme weather scenarios.[7] Other DTCs focus on specific issues, such as smart mobility,[8] citizen feedback,[9] real-time urban drainage models,[10] or flood models.[11] While many technological experiments are underway, the future of building and city-making is undoubtedly digital.

To fully realise the potential of DTCs, it is crucial to address a number of challenges that come with their implementation. One of the foremost challenges is the need for a skilled workforce in multiple disciplines with relevant digital intelligence and data governance expertise.[12] Furthermore, the complexity of data-sharing among various stakeholders in DTCs can often lead to misunderstanding or complications. Additionally, building the technical infrastructure necessary for DTCs requires expertise at the grassroots level with communities as well as desktop work with city managers.[13] This expertise may not be readily available in all cities, particularly in developing regions such as South Africa. Finally, ethical and social considerations must be taken into account to ensure that DTCs are designed and deployed in a manner that benefits all members of society and does not perpetuate existing inequalities. Addressing these challenges will be essential for the successful implementation of DTCs and for creating sustainable and equitable urban futures.

Despite these challenges, the increasing number of DTC initiatives worldwide demonstrates the potential of this technology to revolutionise how we design and manage our cities. Addressing these challenges and incorporating DTC technology into the core education of the built environment disciplines can help close the digital skills gap, propel the development of more intelligent and resilient cities, and contribute to the broader digital intelligence of local communities.

The Future of Cities and the Digital Talent Gap

It is important to take a comprehensive look at the digital talent gap in the built environment, particularly in relation to cities. The urgent challenge of climate crisis and collapse poses the greatest risk to the future of humanity.[14] Regrettably, 21st-century cities are the leading contributors to climate crisis concerns.[15] To effectively address the impact of cities on the climate crisis, it is imperative to leverage technology that can create real-time responsive instruments that can effectively tackle the complexity of urban challenges. It is necessary to evaluate the significance of the digital talent gap in the built environment from this broader perspective.

Despite mounting pressures to address climate change, cities struggle to coordinate efforts and align them with broader climate crisis objectives. This is because climate performance goals within cities are often approached as isolated performance targets, leading to a failure to achieve holistic urban outcomes.[16] However, a siloed approach is insufficient to address the complex nature of climate crisis issues, as emphasised by the broader discourse on "smart cities" and urban sustainability.[17] As such, 21st-century cities are encouraged to adopt a holistic approach to city-making and management, recognising that cities are intricate systems with interrelated and dynamic feedback loops. To achieve this, cities require sophisticated instruments that facilitate the goals of complex systems in real-time. These kinds of city tools are necessarily data-driven and digital. The production and management of such data-driven instruments will require significant amounts of digital human talent, especially from the built environment sector.

As smarter technologies, automation, and cognitive capabilities accelerate, the global demand for digital talent in the workforce continues to grow.[18] To address the global digital talent gap, organisations are embarking on digital transformation journeys or adopting digital skill development strategies. Both native digital organisations (such as software, healthcare, logistics, or financing firms) and non-digital organisations (such as built environment firms) are rapidly deploying digital transformation journeys to remain competitive and prepare for the future of work.[19] Digital transformation can be understood as a process where the implementation of digital technologies and digital capabilities creates transformational effects at scale for organisations and industries alike.[20]

However, there is often a mismatch between the urgency for digital transformation and the practical capacity to implement it effectively. This leads to a significant gap between demand for digital transformation and the ability to service that need. Many digital transformation journeys within organisations fail from the outset, largely due to the lack of both "soft" and "hard" digital skills among ordinary employees. According to a report by Buvat et al. (2017), the vast majority of companies worldwide do not have the necessary digital skills. The gap between what organisations need and the proficiency of their employees is quite large in almost all digital skill categories. Very few companies' training efforts are consistent with their digital strategy at all.[21] Globally, over half (54 percent) of organisations believe that the reason their digital transformation programs fail is because of a lack of digital talent altogether.[22] After all, stewarding, designing, and managing a digital transformation journey in itself is part of the "soft" digital skill set that is grossly lacking in industries at large. While there is an urgency to improve digital technical skills in global employment markets, there is also an urgency to accelerate broad-spectrum digital literacy and intelligence within society overall.[23]

To understand this, it is helpful to look at the impact of the COVID-19 pandemic on workforces. The COVID-19 pandemic has highlighted the urgency for all sectors to prioritise digital skills, including the built environment. Before COVID-19, 90 percent of executives anticipated that digital technologies would disrupt their industries, but only 44 percent believed their organisations were prepared for this disruption at all.[24] After COVID-19, 84 percent of employers say, they have rapidly digitised their processes, including a significant expansion of remote work.[25] The World Economic Forum (WEF) Future of Jobs 2020 Report predicts a 50-50 split between humans and automation in working environments by 2025.

However, the built environment industry has been slow to invest in and adopt digital skills overall, making it particularly vulnerable to such double-disruption scenarios. The rapid pace of technological advancements, including the emergence of ChatGPT4 and other artificial intelligence (AI)-related technologies, is further exacerbating the built environment digital skills gap. To remain competitive and prepare for the future of work, it is critical for the built environment industry to prioritise investment in digital skills training and education. Failure to do so risks falling behind in the race for innovation and losing out on future opportunities for growth and success for projects and people alike.

Against this background, the role of DTs for cities cannot be overstated. The successful implementation of DTs for cities and the broader built environment requires a highly skilled and digital workforce. Without investing in the development of such digital skills, the built environment sector risks falling behind not only in the use of emerging technologies but also in the overall sustainability and survival of 21st-century cities. Therefore, it is essential for the built environment industry to prioritise the development of digital skills and talent to fully leverage the potential of DTs and other emerging technologies.

The Digital Talent Gap in the Built Environment

The digital talent gap remains a significant challenge for the professional service and construction sectors in the built environment.[26] Despite a clear preference for implementing digital technologies, design and construction professionals, companies, institutional bodies, and government agencies in these sectors have struggled to achieve long-term success in digital transformation.[27] There is little evidence demonstrating an adequate understanding of what long-term success of digital transformation means for built environment organisations.[28] In 2017, less than half of built environment firms reported having started a digital transformation journey,[29] and the majority of industry professionals ranked the "digital maturity" of their organisations as very low.[30]

The COVID-19 pandemic has further exposed the limited digital talent pool in the built environment, as organisations were forced to participate in digital project delivery efforts. Both the pandemic and post-pandemic situation further strained the already limited digital-built environment talent pool. As a result, coordination challenges, digital immaturity, and associated difficulties between stakeholders were magnified, revealing a clear lack of alignment in technological ambitions, skills, and capabilities across the industry.[31] As historically siloed actors suddenly had to coordinate digitally in a collaborative way with each other, COVID-19 and fallout activities demonstrate a clear lack of alignment in technological ambitions, skills, and capabilities for the built environment industry at large.[32]

The built environment faces the challenge of retaining traditional talent while also meeting the growing demand for digital skill sets.[33] This has created a significant disparity between rising demands for digital talent and the available talent pool at both the non-professional and professional levels.[34] As a consequence, the built environment industry is falling behind in digital maturity, intelligence, and capabilities, resulting in losses for projects, firms, and individuals.[35]

To address this challenge, built environment organisations must prioritise the development of digital talent, both by investing in upskilling programs for existing employees and by actively recruiting digital natives. The industry must also develop a culture of collaboration and knowledge-sharing to overcome siloed practices and facilitate the adoption of digital technologies. Ultimately, building a robust digital talent pipeline is critical to ensuring the long-term success of the built environment industry in the digital age.

Uncoordinated Digital Talent Development in the Built Environment

The built environment industry is facing a growing skills gap, particularly in "21st-century skills" such as "soft digital skills" and "hard digital skills."[36] As technology continues to transform the industry, it's becoming increasingly important for practitioners to possess a wide range of digital skills. However, many built environment graduates and professionals lack these skills, and upskilling and retraining them can be both time-consuming and expensive for companies. This skills gap is causing frustration for both employers and employees, as it limits the digital talent pool available for hire and decreases project capacity. Without a coordinated effort to address the root causes of this issue, the built environment employment market will continue to suffer.

While we acknowledge many possible causes, the widening skills gap among built environment practitioners, at least in South Africa, can also be traced back to pedagogical causes. Firstly, most built environment education does not emphasise digital competence as a shared core skill. Instead, digital skills are often regarded as standalone skill sets for specialists. Secondly, while shared built environment digital instruments and environments have been successfully deployed at a project level (such as BIM[37] or LeanBIM[38]), most built environment learners do not experience shared, multidisciplinary digital training environments in school. The majority of individuals who join the built environment workforce lack the necessary digital collaboration skills to work effectively with others.

Traditional pedagogy makes it challenging to facilitate shared learning and training environments across built environment disciplines. Each built environment discipline historically focuses on mastering specialist skills, and learners are often only exposed to working together once an actual project begins. On-site learning comes with steep new learning curves, such as developing project coordination skills. The failure to provide relevant digital skill development and shared training experiences is a pedagogical shortcoming that contributes to the widening digital talent gap in the built environment. This digital talent gap encumbers the development and adoption of built environment innovation.

Through our DTC development journey, we have discovered that DTCs present novel prospects for the advancement of digital skills and the creation of collaborative project training environments in the built environment industry. In the subsequent section, we will delve into our DTC development strategy and highlight essential takeaways that should be incorporated into built environment education.

The Hatfield Digital Twin City: Building a Living Urban Laboratory in South Africa

Hatfield is a densely populated urban area located in the heart of the City of Tshwane, South Africa. The region is home to a major inner-city university campus, experimental farms, a range of high-rise and low-rise building stock, and a diverse set of urban functions and activities. Due to its rich urban geography, Hatfield is an ideal location for developing DTCs in Africa, as it provides ample traditional learning opportunities and serves as a valuable case study for this purpose.

The main objective of a DTC is to enhance urban systems, communities, environments, and processes by utilising real-time data feedback loops. Consequently, a well-established DTC requires access to reliable and high-quality urban datasets. However, in South Africa, the quality, consistency, and reliability of urban data vary significantly across different regions. Furthermore, there are several technical and knowledge-related challenges that need to be addressed, including limited access to digital tools, high costs of digital work, frequent power grid disruptions, and significant disparities in digital knowledge, competency, and skill maturity among professionals and the general community.

The Hatfield Digital Twin City Initiative (Figure 2.1) initially faced limitations due to the lack of external funding, resulting in a slower development pace. However, this situation provided us with new educational opportunities. Without funds to purchase data or instruments, we had to find innovative ways to acquire quality urban data while also rethinking our approach to DTC development.

In the subsequent section, we will delve into the valuable insights gained from our DTC development journey and explain how these learnings have impacted our pedagogical works in the built environment.

Lesson 1: Adopt a Bottom-up Digital Twin City Development Approach to Promote Broad-spectrum Digital Skills Development

In South Africa, the absence of dependable open spatial data has been a challenge to DTC development. However, we discovered that this challenge can be turned into a valuable educational opportunity to enhance digital literacy. The first lesson is that DTC development activities can serve as both foreground practices, such as technical development, and background learning opportunities, including traditional learning objectives, in digital built environment education.

The use of cloud-based tools such as BIM, Internet of Things (IoT), and GeoBIM has made it possible for experts to create basic DTCs using existing data or skills. However, an expert-led approach to their development has

Digital Twin Cities 33

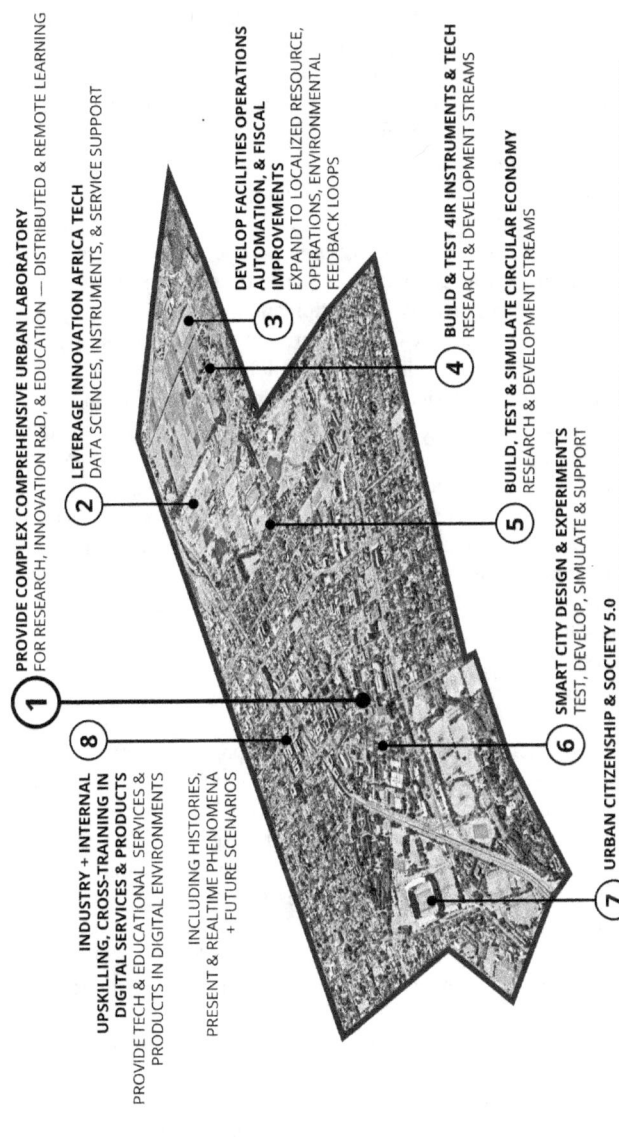

Figure 2.1 The Hatfield Digital Twin City is approximately twenty-square-kilometre digital development area in South Africa.

Source: Davey 2024a.

created a misconception that these processes are exclusive to experts. This approach has resulted in a high dependency on experts to manage development processes and has impeded the adoption of fundamental digital skills and practices in the broader built environment community. It is important to note that many basic DTC development activities are user-friendly and accessible to non-experts. Rather than focusing solely on creating digital products, we believe that DTC development should be viewed as an opportunity to create digital learning processes that can serve as training grounds for a broad spectrum of built environment digital education.

Rather than utilising a conventional expert-driven methodology, we implemented a transdisciplinary, bottom-up learning approach that prioritised inclusivity. This approach involves engaging individuals at various levels and from diverse backgrounds to actively participate and contribute to the learning process. It encourages collaboration and knowledge-sharing from the ground level, allowing a wide range of perspectives and insights to shape the learning experience rather than relying solely on experts, authorities, or teachers to dictate the curriculum. This approach enabled us to exploit the technical DTC development process while creating novel educational opportunities. Firstly, learners had the chance to generate base urban datasets themselves, which fostered the acquisition of new digital and data skills among learners. Secondly, this approach enabled built environment learners to participate in DTC development processes alongside other disciplines, regardless of their proficiency or previous experience in the digital realm. The shift in pedagogical focus from solely developing discipline-specific digital skills to promoting collective digital skill development resulted in collaborative project training experiences for diverse built environment teams, thus fostering inclusive and comprehensive digital learning.

Our approach to aligning day-to-day learning activities with DTC development requirements has proved successful in producing *geometric* and *process* data from student assignments. We were also able to issue scalable digital tasks to fill missing datasets for the DTC. This strategy not only helped us quickly acquire urban data but also provided students with direct opportunities to learn digitisation and data-collection skills alongside their regular built environment education activities (see Figure 2.2). By prioritising digital learning *processes* over digital *products*, we are creating a more inclusive approach to DTC development, which can accelerate the adoption of fundamental digital skills and practices in the built environment community.

For example, to overcome the challenge of the lack of open spatial data, we took action by providing basic open Geographic Information System (GIS) training to first-year architecture students and third-year construction economics students. We tasked students with populating building footprints and digital site plans to build base DTC data as part of basic learning assignments. To ensure that these skills were not only limited to a select few courses,

Digital Twin Cities 35

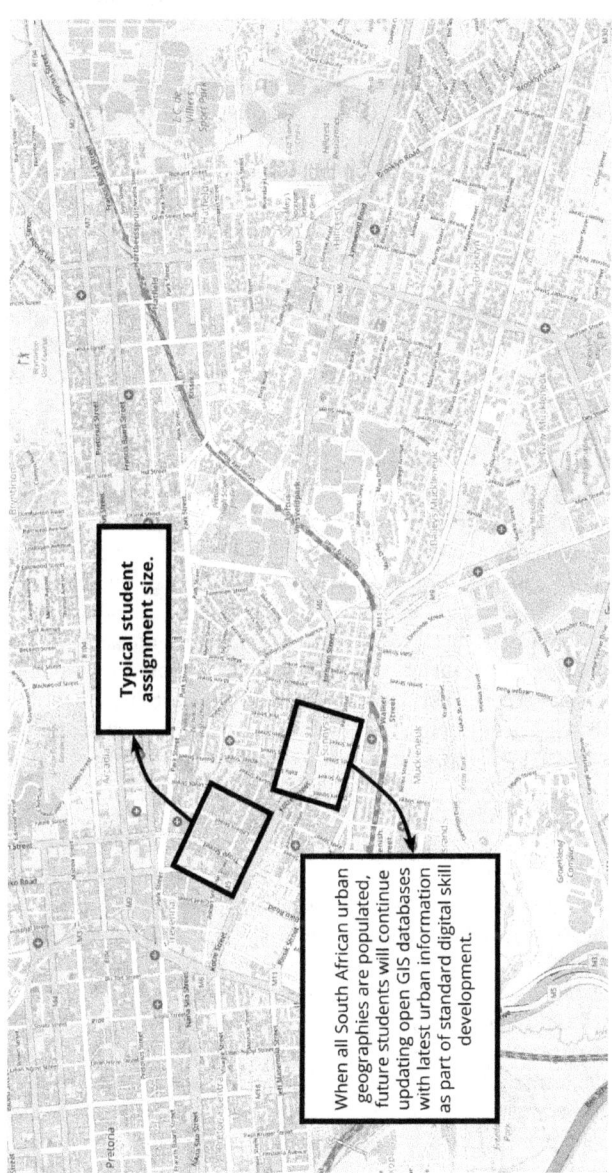

Figure 2.2 Coupling foreground digital twin city development activities directly to background learning activities, students were tasked to map formal and informal South African urban areas through OpenStreetMap.

Source: Davey 2024b.

we incorporated digital spatial assessment and data-driven outcomes into our design studios' education experiences. By doing so, we engaged hundreds of students, regardless of their background, skills, or prior experience, in basic DTC data production.

To illustrate our approach, we incorporated digital mapping exercises into the curriculum for first-year Earth Sciences students. Using OpenStreetMap, students mapped their home neighbourhoods, a basic built environment skill. We also assigned third-year construction economics students to map commercial blocks, which is also a basic skill but with an added challenge of assessing sustainability and performance objectives for the blocks they mapped, an advanced skill. These educational activities were initiated during the COVID-19 pandemic and have since become an integral part of our curriculum. By participating in these activities, students gain hands-on experience in digital skills while also advancing their knowledge in the built environment field. Moreover, their contributions to local digital urban datasets provide valuable insights for the development of a more accurate DTC.

By integrating digital skills as part of the core curriculum across all built environment disciplines, we were able to sow the seeds of digital proficiency among an entire generation of graduates. As a result, we have observed a growing interest in digital tools and techniques not only among architecture students but also in other departments within the built environment field. For instance, in 2022, quantity surveying students showed a keen interest in exploring scan-to-BIM alongside architecture students. This collaborative effort proved to be a success, paving the way for structural engineering and quantity surveying students to join the effort in 2023 as they explored scan-to-BIM for urban material mining. This cross-disciplinary approach has allowed us to foster a shared digital language and maturity across all our built environment departments, promoting a more inclusive and collaborative approach to digital skill development.

The integration of digital skills into core-built environment education has led to sustainable and long-term impacts on the students' learning and development. Despite the origins of these activities during the COVID-19 pandemic, the students have continued to build upon their digital skills, contributing to the growth of digital appetites and a shared digital language across various built environment departments. For instance, the first-year students who mapped their home neighbourhoods in OpenStreetMap in 2020 are now in their third year, using their existing digital maps to layer in detailed building stock characteristics, thereby showcasing the potential of continuous or layered digital learning. This approach to digital education has planted seeds of digital talent across generations of built environment graduates and opened up new possibilities (such as urban material mining through scan-to-BIM skills training). It is evident that the integration of digital skills into core-built environment education can lead to ongoing digital learning and development, ultimately driving sustainable and long-term impacts.

Digital Twin Cities 37

Figure 2.3 Foreground education meets digital city development, as students create two improved transportation designs in two days, leveraging their shared digital intelligence.

Source: Davey 2024c.

Redefining digital twinning from a *product* to an ongoing *process* unlocks new opportunities for vertical integration among learners. For example, in our department, we host an ice-breaker activity called *Vertical Studio* at the beginning of every academic year to promote inclusivity and participation among the student body. During *Vertical Studio*, hybrid teams are formed across different year groups (vertical) rather than within year groups (horizontal) to create physical design projects that will be integrated into a larger site as part of the supergroup. This process teaches leadership and coordination skills while also giving opportunity for knowledge transfer and socialising across the student body.

In 2023, the *Vertical Studio* challenge was to improve Hatfield's transportation system. We opened the Hatfield Digital Twin City platform so that all year groups could quickly build off the same digital environment instantly, and students had only three days to produce a physical design solution from start to finish. Due to the historic digital pedagogical efforts in digital mapping skills, older students were already comfortable working with a shared digital mindset, and the entire physical design model was constructed twice in only two days. As a result, we plan to develop two *Vertical Studio* activities each year – one physical and one digital – to inform both the physical and digital education of our students. These annual *Vertical Studios* are not only important foreground activities for students to bond together on but also important background digital development activities in the process of digital twinning of Hatfield.

Lesson 2: High-end Technological Solutions Are Often Less Valuable than Broad-spectrum Human Learning

South African urban settings are characterised by complex and diverse landscapes, consisting of a mix of medium-to-high-density formal and informal settlements (as shown in Figures 2.4 and 2.5). However, due to the rapid pace of change and limited documentation, many areas remain largely undocumented, with only aerial photography as a source of information. In our initial attempts to develop a DTC, we focused on deploying high-end technological solutions such as AI and machine learning (ML) GIS models to reproduce spatial geometries for these undocumented areas. However, this approach proved to be challenging and time-consuming, with many errors and limited value being produced despite the investment of machine hours and months of human learning and production time. Moreover, AI/ML models are limited in their ability to capture "soft" or contextual urban information. Eventually, progress was made with AI/ML models, but by then, the urban landscape had already changed significantly, rendering our initial "advanced technical efforts" somewhat fruitless.

Although technically advanced, the AI/ML approach had several practical shortcomings. The steep learning curve for AI/ML, combined with additional

Figure 2.4 The complex and fast-paced urban growth of the Melusi informal settlement.

Source: Department of Architecture, University of Pretoria, South Africa. Postgraduate student works, 2022.

technological constraints in South Africa (such as consistent access to sophisticated software, high-end technology, advanced digital education, consistent power, and data bandwidth limitations), is unrealistic. Creating DTCs in South Africa that rely on such assumptions would only widen the technological divide, create digital inequity, and introduce more barriers than opportunities. Using high-end technological approaches is an exclusionary process that defeats our long-term objectives. Therefore, we turned towards education processes as a more inclusive solution.

Instead of relying on high-end technological solutions, we adopted an educational approach that proved to be more effective and efficient. By assigning open GIS projects to design and construction economics students, we were able to document several square kilometres of South African environments in open Hatfield. The geography was mapped in less than a week, which allowed us to move to other geographies. This student task required only three hours per student in a dedicated area, in contrast to the more than two months it took for the AI/ML approach. Furthermore, by participating in these projects, students gained hands-on experience in producing basic digital urban datasets. Compared to the AI/ML approach, this educational approach reduced spatial errors as students took care to produce accurate results for their assignments.

This approach resulted in several learning outcomes. First, all participating built environment students developed a shared digital spatial skill and language. Second, this data is administered on international servers, allowing students to work synchronously or asynchronously, eliminating local technological impediments (such as expensive software, power cuts, data loss or theft, or COVID-19 restrictions). Third, students were pleased and satisfied to learn "novel" yet replicable digital skills independent of local technical

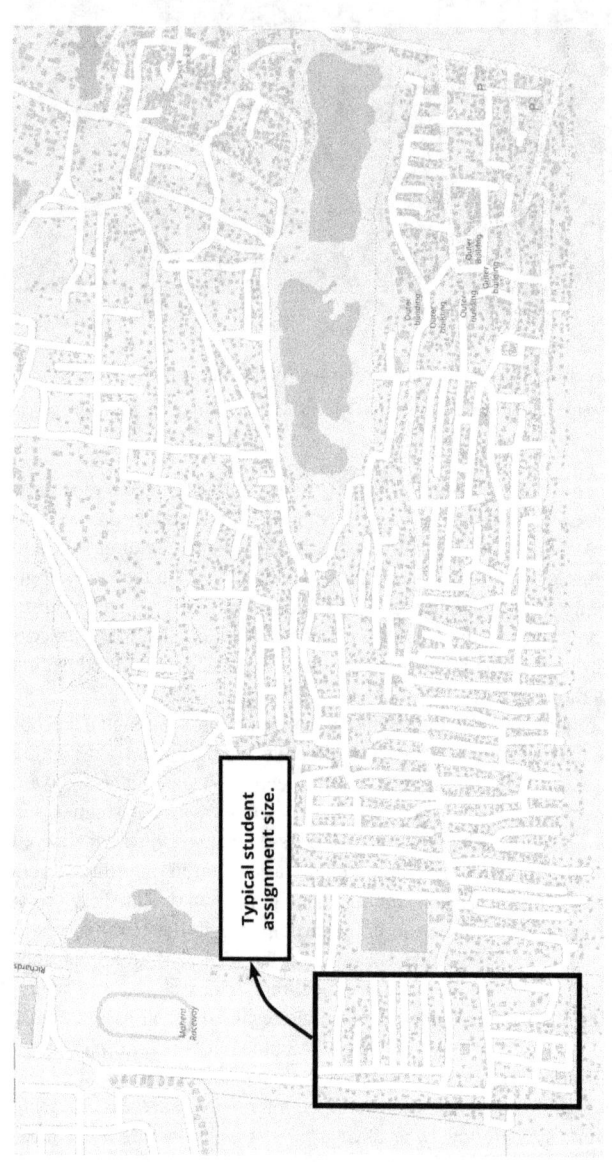

Figure 2.5 The open GIS mapping results from the 2022 Informal Settlement Climate Adaption Studio.
Source: Department of Architecture, University of Pretoria, South Africa. Postgraduate student works, 2022.

difficulties. The assignments were adjusted so participants could populate spatial data for any geography. This way, international students from Zimbabwe, Botswana, Namibia, and other African territories communally contributed to updating their home environments while in South African schools. Some students transferred this skill to their local communities or work environments.

Lesson 3: Transdisciplinary Works Are Prerequisites for and Results of Building Digital Twin Cities

Any DT must have a purpose, which we call a *use-case*. A "use-case" describes a specific scenario or situation where a product or system is applied to achieve specific goals. For example, in the context of a ride-sharing app, a *use-case* could be a passenger booking a ride, including the steps involved from requesting a ride to reaching the destination. For the Hatfield Digital Twin City, we focused on on-campus water consumption as a first *use-case* experiment. We digitised the university buildings' operational water data to produce a real-time water consumption behaviour dashboard. While much detail is still needed to benchmark this work, we constructed a rudimentary *water twin*.

Initially, the *water twin* had a technical focus. The team included an architect, a facility operations system engineer, and a data scientist. Meanwhile, university-wide interest in DT technology was growing. Eventually, the chemical engineering faculty asked the architecture faculty: could we use the real-time *water twin* data to train chemical engineering students in AI/ML applications? As part of their technical work experience requirements, a dozen chemical engineering students participated in *water twin* development, training themselves on AI/ML from real-time water data.

As a result of this transdisciplinary engagement, the *water twin* technical experiment grew beyond its initial purpose of monitoring on-campus water consumption. Chemical engineering students leveraged the real-time data to train themselves on AI/ML applications, leading to the development of creative urban concept projects such as a *Campus Water Utility Prediction App*, *Hatfield Zero-Waste Project*, and *Hatfield Alternative Net-Zero Urban Energy* projects (Figure 2.6). This approach allowed diverse students to work on urban topics from new perspectives that they are not typically exposed to in their standard curricula, resulting in unique and innovative ideas.

Similarly, students from other disciplines, such as geography, quantity surveying, civil engineering, and architecture, also contributed to Hatfield Digital Twin City works, learning how to create 3D point-cloud-to-GeoBIM models and protocols (Figure 2.7) together. By focusing on shared outcomes of DTC development goals, students engaged in simultaneous learning with diverse disciplines, borrowing skills from each other to achieve specific DTC *use-cases*. This collaborative and interdisciplinary approach not only enhances the learning experience for students but also helps to create more holistic and effective DT solutions.

Figure 2.6 Exam project outcomes from chemical engineering students working with the architecture department on urban topics using digital twin city data for AI/ML training.

Source: Davey 2024d.

In conclusion, the development of DTCs requires a transdisciplinary approach that involves diverse expertise and perspectives. The Hatfield Digital Twin City project exemplifies this approach, with the water twin experiment expanding beyond its initial purpose and involving students from various disciplines such as chemical engineering, geography, quantity surveying, civil

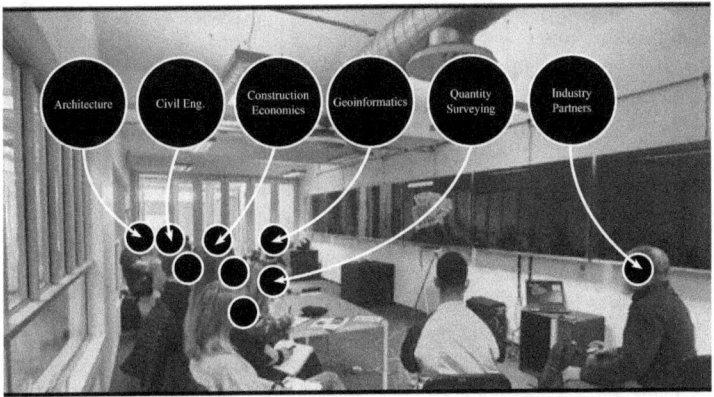

Figure 2.7 Transdisciplinary shared digital learning to create digital twin city geometric data works.

Source: Department of Architecture, University of Pretoria, South Africa. Postgraduate student works, 2022.

engineering, and architecture. The collaborative effort resulted in unique and innovative ideas and enhanced the students' learning experience while achieving specific DTC use-cases. This approach highlights the importance of shared outcomes and simultaneous learning across diverse disciplines to create more effective and holistic DT solutions.

Lesson 4: Building Shared Digital Talent Does Not Eliminate Core Competencies

The concept of a DT involves creating real-time feedback loops between the physical world and data streams. However, the definition of "real-time" data varies depending on the specific use-case. For instance, creating a *water-consumption* DT would require different real-time data collection intervals than a *community water-use* DT. A *water-consumption* DT could focus on detecting and reducing infrastructure water leakages, necessitating measurement of water flow data in seconds or minutes. On the other hand, a *community water-use* DT would aim to improve individual or household water-use behaviour, requiring not only water flow data (measured in minutes) but also a more nuanced understanding of community behaviour over several days or seasons. However, obtaining reliable long-term fine-grain community datasets are often sensitive and very scarce, especially in South Africa.

This situation provides another digital learning opportunity. In the context of our design studio pedagogy, social impact and community engagement are crucial areas of focus. However, the lack of standard practices for generating digital community fieldwork datasets meant that valuable fine-grain community information was frequently lost or unavailable for longitudinal use. To address this challenge, we have reconfigured our design studios to include real-time field GIS mapping as part of community and site investigation work. This has resulted in the development of the *ukuDoba Method*[39] by architecture and geography students, which enables any student, regardless of their discipline, to learn and perform community GIS data collection in open-source ways with real-time results. This collaborative approach not only enhances the acquisition of cross-disciplinary digital skills but also plays a crucial role in building comprehensive DT datasets for urban development and sustainability.

For instance, student teams working on a food mapping project might use the *ukuDoba Method* to gather information about local food sources, such as farmers' markets, grocery stores, and community gardens. They could collect data on the types of produce available, prices, and opening hours, creating a comprehensive map that helps residents find fresh, affordable food options in their neighbourhood. In the context of community leadership mapping, students employing the *ukuDoba Method* could collect fine-grain local data on community leaders, including their names, roles, and contributions to local initiatives. By mapping this information, residents can better understand the individuals driving positive change in their community and potentially identify opportunities for collaboration and support. The *ukuDoba Method* also allows for the collection of non-traditional data, such as drawings or soundscapes, which can be stored in a centralised database for longitudinal and multidisciplinary use.

The *ukuDoba Method* is a valuable tool in transient, fast-changing, or complex urban environments, particularly in informal settlements where community concerns are often poorly documented for long-term learning. By using this method, architecture students were able to capture important fine-grain community data, such as changes in informal streets, occupancy conditions, community sentiment shifts, drawings, and interpretations, and nuanced information like why water sources relocated to new places. This approach enables new students to understand the histories of informal communities faster, contribute new layers of data, and develop higher-quality spatial design responses (Figure 2.8). Moreover, this data is easily accessible to other disciplines, allowing for quick sharing of fine-grain community information between design, public health, and food security students. This method not only provides a valuable digital learning opportunity but also enhances core learning competencies while improving community engagement and generating valuable data for future use. Students who had rich microdata could produce much more relevant and contextual design solutions (Figure 2.9). The lesson that we learned was that building shared digital talent doesn't necessarily replace the core learning competencies, but it has the potential to enhance them.

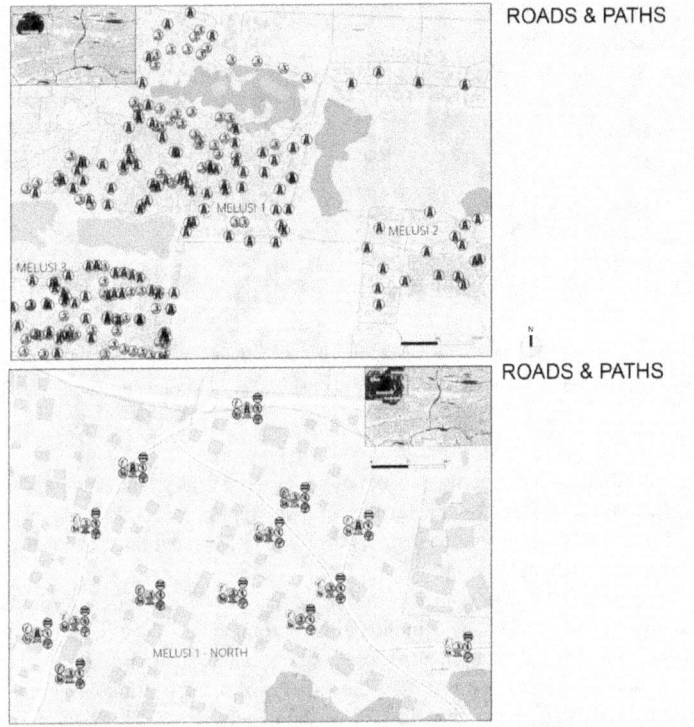

Figure 2.8 Building open GIS spatial histories for fast-changing informal urban environments.

Source: Department of Architecture, University of Pretoria, South Africa. Postgraduate student works, 2022.

Conclusion: Digital Twin Cities Are Vehicles for Redefining the Value of Digital Skills in Built Environment Pedagogy

Urban DT technology has the potential to revolutionise urban living and work, offering exciting opportunities for improving urban areas' sustainability and residents' quality of life. However, there are significant challenges, including data-sharing complexities, a shortage of digital skills, and the need for inclusivity and ethical considerations in local contexts. To achieve a future where DTCs are the norm, fostering a culture of learning, collaboration, and digital skill development is essential, especially in the built environment sector. Educators can play a pivotal role in addressing the digital skills gap by integrating DTC development processes into core curriculum, benefiting learners,

Figure 2.9 Student design responses for 2022 Melusi Climate Adaption Studio.

Source: Department of Architecture, University of Pretoria, South Africa. Postgraduate student works, 2022.

and contributing to achieving the goal of widespread DTCs. The chapter also highlighted the importance of a transdisciplinary approach in addressing these challenges and offers valuable insights for other cities and industries looking to embrace the digital revolution.

The Hatfield Digital Twin City Initiative has provided valuable insights into how pedagogical changes in the built environment can be effectively integrated with DTC development. These insights can be summarised into four key lessons. Lesson 1 demonstrates the success of incorporating day-to-day learning activities that align with DTC development needs. This bottom-up approach not only facilitates the acquisition of urban data through student assignments but also nurtures digitisation and data-collection skills within the context of the built environment education. Lesson 2 highlights the significance of prioritising comprehensive human learning over high-tech solutions. It emphasises the development of shared digital spatial skills and international collaboration, reducing technological barriers and enabling students to gain novel digital competencies. Lesson 3 underscores the essential role of transdisciplinary collaboration in the creation of DTCs. It shows that diverse expertise and perspectives from various disciplines are crucial to building effective and holistic DT solutions. Lastly, Lesson 4 reveals that fostering shared digital talent complements rather than replaces core competencies. It enhances the learning experience, encourages community engagement, and generates valuable data while improving core competencies in the built environment field. Collectively, these lessons promote a holistic approach that aligns pedagogical changes with DTC development, fostering inclusivity, digital skill acquisition, and community-centred solutions while enhancing core competencies.

However, the built environment digital talent gap is a significant challenge that must be addressed urgently, especially concerning cities. The urgency of the climate crisis highlights the need for sophisticated instruments to facilitate the goals of complex systems, like cities, in real time. To achieve this, cities must adopt a holistic approach to city-making and management, recognising that cities are intricate systems with interrelated feedback loops. However, a lack of digital skills and talent is hindering the adoption and implementation of emerging technologies, such as DTs, which are necessary for addressing these challenges. The COVID-19 pandemic has further highlighted the need for all sectors, including the built environment, to prioritise digital skills. Therefore, it is critical for the built environment industry to prioritise investment in digital skills training and education to remain competitive and prepare for the future of work.

The potential of DTC technology to revolutionise the built environment industry is vast. DTs for cities offer a platform for extensive learning and skills development, which can help to bridge the digital talent gap and enhance the sustainability and resilience of urban areas. However, successful implementation of DTCs requires a collaborative effort from all stakeholders, particularly built environment educators, to develop both hard and soft digital skills among people. By fostering a culture of transdisciplinary learning and collaboration through the production of local DTCs, we can unlock the full transformative potential of DTCs and create a future where they are the norm.

To bridge the growing digital talent gap in the built environment and adapt to the increasing trend towards digitalisation in buildings and cities, educators need to re-evaluate how they instil collaborative digital practices from the foundational level. The built environment community must embrace a shared digital mindset and recognise digital skills as core competencies rather than peripheral skills to meet the demand for digital skills. These skills need to be developed concurrently with other core competencies without hindering their progress. Recognising digitisation practices as a minimum core and shared built environment skill is essential for relevant and up-to-date education. DTC development activities can provide such educational opportunities by reframing digitisation practices as essential background activities in built environment education. Direct participation in DTC development enables graduates to learn meaningfully and support coordinated skill development as a built environment community.

While the end goal of developing DTCs as a *product* is certainly beneficial, it's important not to overlook the value of seeing the *process* itself as an opportunity for ongoing learning and skill development. By engaging in the creation and maintenance of DTCs, individuals and communities can develop a broad range of digital skills, including data management, analysis, and visualisation, as well as gain a deeper understanding of complex systems and urban environments. Additionally, this process-oriented approach allows for ongoing experimentation and iteration, creating a space for continuous learning and improvement. Ultimately, by viewing DTCs as a *process* rather than simply a *product*, we can unlock their full potential as a tool for broad-spectrum digital skill development and innovation in the built environment.

Basic DTC development activities can be done for free or at minimal costs, making it accessible to learners with varying skill levels. Incorporating DTC development as a background pedagogical practice can promote the development of shared multi-scalar learnable, transferable, and interchangeable skill sets among learners, which are essential for transdisciplinary engagement. DTC data generation can also provide practical interdisciplinary learning and transdisciplinary training opportunities. By integrating DTC development as a background practice, learners can develop these skills without hindering their core competencies.

Moreover, transdisciplinary engagement is a prerequisite and an outcome of DTC efforts, creating valuable two-way learning opportunities for participants. The production of DTCs by both experts and new learners fosters the development of a digital urban commons, generating a shared learning environment where knowledge and skills can be quickly transferred. Therefore, incorporating DTC development efforts as a background pedagogical practice can create an inclusive and collaborative learning environment that fosters the development of valuable and transferable skills.

In conclusion, addressing the digital talent gap in the built environment sector is crucial for cities to achieve their sustainability and resilience goals in real time. DTCs offer a transformative solution to this challenge, providing a platform for extensive learning and skill development. However, successful implementation requires a collaborative effort from all stakeholders, particularly built environment educators, to develop both hard and soft digital skills among people. By embracing a shared digital mindset, viewing DTCs as a process for ongoing learning, and integrating development efforts as a background pedagogical practice, we can create a culture of transdisciplinary learning and collaboration that fosters the development of valuable and transferable skills. By prioritising digital skills and adopting a transdisciplinary approach, the built environment industry can fully leverage the potential of emerging technologies for the overall sustainability and survival of 21st-century cities.

Notes

1 Zaheer Allam and David S. Jones, "Future (Post-COVID) Digital, Smart and Sustainable Cities in the Wake of 6G: Digital Twins, Immersive Realities and New Urban Economies," *Land Use Policy* 101 (2021): 105201, https://doi.org/https://doi.org/10.1016/j.landusepol.2020.105201; Eleni Papadonikolaki, Ilias Krystallis, and Bethan Morgan, "Digital Technologies in Built Environment Projects: Review and Future Directions," *Project Management Journal* 53, no. 5 (February 2022): 501–19, https://doi.org/10.1177/87569728211070225; Armstrong Geno, Gilge Clay, and Kevin Max, "No Turning Back. An Industry Ready to Transcend: 2021

Global Construction Survey," 2021, https://assets.kpmg/content/dam/kpmg/xx/pdf/2021/08/global-construction-survey1.pdf.

2 Allam and Jones, "Future (Post-COVID) Digital, Smart and Sustainable Cities in the Wake of 6G."; Bart Brink and Casey Rutland, "Take BIM Processes to the next Level with Digital Twins," BuildingSmart International, June 2020, https://blog.buildingsmart.org/blog/take-bim-processes-to-the-next-level-with-digital-twins; Andrés Camero and Enrique Alba, "Smart City and Information Technology: A Review," *Cities* 93 (2019): 84–94, https://doi.org/10.1016/j.cities.2019.04.014; Juan Manuel Davila Delgado and Lukumon Oyedele, "Digital Twins for the Built Environment: Learning from Conceptual and Process Models in Manufacturing," *Advanced Engineering Informatics* 49 (August 2021): 101332, https://doi.org/10.1016/j.aei.2021.101332; Bernd Ketzler et al., "Digital Twins for Cities: A State of the Art Review," *Built Environment* 46, no. 4 (December 2020): 547–73, https://doi.org/10.2148/BENV.46.4.547; Jair Ribeiro, "The Digital Transformation Passes through the Digital Twins.," October 2020, https://medium.com/predict/the-digital-transformation-passes-through-the-digital-twins-560804cf86d6; Gary White et al., "A Digital Twin Smart City for Citizen Feedback," *Cities* 110 (2021): 103064, https://doi.org/10.1016/j.cities.2020.103064.

3 National Research Foundation, "Virtual Singapore," Government of Singapore, 2018, https://www.sla.gov.sg/articles/press-releases/2014/virtual-singapore-a-3d-city-model-platform-for-knowledge-sharing-and-community-collaboration.

4 Buidmedia, "Wellington Digital Twin" (Wellingon, New Zealand, 2021), https://buildmedia.com/work/wellington-digital-twin.

5 Chalmers University of Technology, "Digital Twin Cities Centre," A Vinnova competence centre, 2020, https://dtcc.chalmers.se/.

6 Buidmedia, "Wellington Digital Twin."

7 Anja Hopfstock et al., "Building a Digital Twin for Germany. Using Large-Scale, High-Resolution Lidar to Support Policymakers," GIM International, March 2022, https://www.gim-international.com/content/article/building-a-digital-twin-for-germany.

8 Ahyun Lee et al., "A Geospatial Platform to Manage Large-scale Individual Mobility for an Urban Digital Twin Platform," *Remote Sensing* 14, no. 3 (2022): 723, https://doi.org/10.3390/rs14030723.

9 White et al., "A Digital Twin Smart City for Citizen Feedback."

10 Matthew Bartos and Branko Kerkez, "Pipedream: An Interactive Digital Twin Model for Natural and Urban Drainage Systems," *Environmental Modelling and Software* 144 (October 2021): 105120, https://doi.org/10.1016/j.envsoft.2021.105120.

11 Robert Mankowski, "City-Scale Digital Twins for Flood Resilience," February 2020, https://www.gim-international.com/content/article/city-scale-digital-twins-for-flood-resilience.

12 Muhammad Shahzad et al., "Digital Twins in Built Environments: An Investigation of the Characteristics, Applications, and Challenges," *Buildings* 12, no. 2 (2022): 120, https://doi.org/10.3390/buildings12020120; Jaume Ferré-Bigorra, Miquel Casals, and Marta Gangolells, "The Adoption of Urban Digital Twins," *Cities* 131 (December 2022): 103905, https://doi.org/10.1016/j.cities.2022.103905; Ketzler et al., "Digital Twins for Cities."

13 Sharon Zukin, "Seeing like a City: How Tech Became Urban," *Theory and Society* 49, no. 5–6 (October 1, 2020): 941–64, https://doi.org/10.1007/s11186-020-09410-4.

14 World Economic Forum, "The Future of Jobs Report 2020," *The Future of Jobs Report*, October 2020, https://www.weforum.org/reports/the-future-of-jobs-report-2020/.

15 UN-Habitat, "World Cities Report 2020 - The Value of Sustainable Urbanization," *Sereal Untuk*, 2020, https://unhabitat.org/sites/default/files/2020/10/wcr_2020_report.pdf.

16 Kate Raworth, *Doughnut Economics* (Chlesea Green Publishing, Vermont, USA, 2018).
17 Fang Zhao et al., "Smart City Research: A Holistic and State-of-the-art Literature Review," *Cities* 119 (December 2021): 103406, https://doi.org/10.1016/j.cities.2021.103406.
18 KPMG International et al., "No Turning Back. An Industry Ready to Transcend: 2021 Global Construction Survey," 2021, https://assets.kpmg/content/dam/kpmg/xx/pdf/2021/08/global-construction-survey1.pdf; Armstrong Geno and Gilge Clay, "Make It, or Break It. Reimagining Governance, People and Technology in the Construction Industry: Global Construction Survey 2017," *KPMG International*, 2017, https://assets.kpmg/content/dam/kpmg/xx/pdf/2017/10/global-construction-survey-make-it-or-break-it.pdf.
19 Barbara Spitzer et al., "The Digital Talent Gap: Developing Skills for Today's Digital Organizations," *Capgemini Consulting and MIT The Centre for Digital Business*, 2013, 1–13, https://library.iated.org/view/SPITZER2015DIG; World Economic Forum, "The Future of Jobs Report 2020."
20 Ayokunle O. Olanipekun and Monty Sutrisna, "Facilitating Digital Transformation in Construction—A Systematic Review of the Current State of the Art," *Frontiers in Built Environment* 7 (2021): 96, https://doi.org/10.3389/fbuil.2021.660758.
21 Jerome Buvat et al., "The Digital Talent Gap: Are Companies Doing Enough?" *Capgemini and LinkedIn*, 2017, 40, https://www.capgemini.com/insights/research-library/; Marcella M. Bonanomi et al., "The Impact of Digital Transformation on Formal and Informal Organizational Structures of Large Architecture and Engineering Firms," *Engineering, Construction and Architectural Management* 27, no. 4 (2020): 872–92, https://doi.org/10.1108/ECAM-03-2019-0119.
22 Buvat et al., "The Digital Talent Gap"
23 Ibid.; Gerald C. Kane et al., "Aligning the Organization for Its Digital Future," *MIT-Sloan Management Review*, no. 58180 (July 2016): 1–29, https://sloanreview.mit.edu/projects/aligning-for-digital-future/; Rubén Mancha and Ganesan Shankaranarayanan, "Making a Digital Innovator: Antecedents of Innovativeness with Digital Technologies," *Information Technology and People* 34, no. 1 (2021): 318–35, https://doi.org/10.1108/ITP-12-2018-0577; Joe Speicher et al., "Supporting Worker Success in the Age of Automation." (2019), https://www2.deloitte.com/content/dam/Deloitte/us/Documents/monitor-institute/us-monitor-institute-supporting-worker-success-in-the-age-of-automation.pdf; Spitzer et al., "The Digital Talent Gap"; World Economic Forum, "The Future of Jobs Report 2020."
24 Kane et al., "Aligning the Organization for Its Digital Future."
25 World Economic Forum, "The Future of Jobs Report 2020."
26 UK Construction Media, "Integrating Digital Skills in Construction," March 2022, https://www.ukconstructionmedia.co.uk/features/integrating-digital-skills-in-construction/; KPMG International et al., "No Turning Back"; Olanipekun and Sutrisna, "Facilitating Digital Transformation in Construction"; UNEP, "2020 Global Status Report for Buildings and Construction," *Global Status Report*, Nairobi, 2020, 20–24, www.globalabc.org; World Economic Forum, "The Future of Jobs Report 2020."
27 Laila Mohamed Khodeir and Ashraf Ali Nessim, "Changing Skills for Architecture Students Employability: Analysis of Job Market versus Architecture Education in Egypt," *Ain Shams Engineering Journal* 11, no. 3 (2020): 811–21, https://doi.org/https://doi.org/10.1016/j.asej.2019.11.006; Olanipekun and Sutrisna, "Facilitating Digital Transformation in Construction"; UNEP, "2020 Global Status Report for Buildings and Construction."
28 Olanipekun and Sutrisna, "Facilitating Digital Transformation in Construction."
29 Geno and Clay, "Make It, or Break It."

30 Ibid.
31 Ayyoob Sharifi and Amir Reza Khavarian-Garmsir, "The COVID-19 Pandemic: Impacts on Cities and Major Lessons for Urban Planning, Design, and Management," *Science of the Total Environment* 749 (2020), https://doi.org/10.1016/j.scitotenv.2020.142391; Allam and Jones, "Future (Post-COVID) Digital, Smart and Sustainable Cities in the Wake of 6G."; Marsh McLennan, SK Group, and Zurich Insurance Group, *The Global Risks Report 2021*, *Weforum.Org*, 2021, https://www.weforum.org/reports/the-global-risks-report-2021.
32 KPMG International et al., "No Turning Back."
33 Speicher et al., "Supporting Worker Success in the Age of Automation"; KPMG International et al., "No Turning Back."
34 KPMG International et al. ""No Turning Back."; Deloitte, "Africa Construction Trends Report 2020. Managing Supply Chain Risk and Disruption in Capital Projects," 2020, https://www2.deloitte.com/content/dam/Deloitte/za/Documents/energy-resources/za-Africa-Construction-Trends-2020-Final.pdf; Speicher et al., "Supporting Worker Success in the Age of Automation."
35 Rajat Agarwal, Shankar Chandrasekaran, and Mukund Sridhar, "Imagining Construction's Digital Future: Capital Projects and Infrastructure" (Singapore, June 2016), https://www.mckinsey.com/~/media/mckinsey/business%20functions/operations/our%20insights/imagining%20constructions%20digital%20future/imagining-constructions-digital-future.pdf; KPMG International et al., "No Turning Back"; Geno and Clay, "Make It, or Break It."; Khodeir and Nessim, "Changing Skills for Architecture Students Employability"; Kevin Rooney, "BIM Education. Global 2017 Update Report," May 2017, https://www.bimalliance.se/library/3041/bim_education_global_2017_update_report_v40.pdf; Padil Suhaili, Esa. Ahmad, and Mohamed Jamal Abidah. Ainah, "Soft Skills Construct for Architecture Graduate in Accordance with Industries Requirement," *International Journal of Humanities, Arts and Social Sciences* 1, no. 3 (October 2015): 119–23, https://kkgpublications.com/wp-content/uploads/2019/04/IJHSS.20002-3.pdf; UNEP, "2020 Global Status Report for Buildings and Construction."
36 KPMG International et al., "No Turning Back"; Khodeir and Nessim, "Changing Skills for Architecture Students Employability"; Deloitte, "Africa Construction Trends Report 2020"; Suhaili, Ahmad, and Ainah, "Soft Skills Construct for Architecture Graduate in Accordance with Industries Requirement"; UNEP, "2020 Global Status Report for Buildings and Construction."
37 Amarnath Chegu Badrinath, Yun Tsui Chang, and Shang Hsien Hsieh, "A Review of Tertiary BIM Education for Advanced Engineering Communication with Visualization," *Visualization in Engineering*, July 2016, https://doi.org/10.1186/s40327-016-0038-6.
38 Felipe Mellado and Eric C. W. Lou, "Building Information Modelling, Lean and Sustainability: An Integration Framework to Promote Performance Improvements in the Construction Industry," *Sustainable Cities and Society* 61 (2020): 102255, https://doi.org/https://doi.org/10.1016/j.scs.2020.102355.
39 Department of Architecture, *The UkuDoba Method: A Methodological Framework for Effective Data Collection and Storage.*, ed. Calayde Davey, Version 3 (City of Tshwane: University of Pretoria and Chalmers University of Technology, 2020).

Bibliography

Agarwal, Rajat, Shankar Chandrasekaran, and Mukund Sridhar. "Imagining Construction's Digital Future: Capital Projects and Infrastructure." Singapore, June 2016. https://www.mckinsey.com/~/media/mckinsey/business%20functions/operations/

our%20insights/imagining%20constructions%20digital%20future/imagining-constructions-digital-future.pdf.

Allam, Zaheer, and David S. Jones. "Future (Post-COVID) Digital, Smart and Sustainable Cities in the Wake of 6G: Digital Twins, Immersive Realities and New Urban Economies." *Land Use Policy* 101 (2021): 105201. https://doi.org/10.1016/j.landusepol.2020.105201.

Bartos, Matthew, and Branko Kerkez. "Pipedream: An Interactive Digital Twin Model for Natural and Urban Drainage Systems." *Environmental Modelling and Software* 144 (October 2021): 105120. https://doi.org/10.1016/j.envsoft.2021.105120.

Bonanomi, Marcella M., Daniel M. Hall, Sheryl Staub-French, Aubrey Tucker, and Cinzia Maria Luisa Talamo. "The Impact of Digital Transformation on Formal and Informal Organizational Structures of Large Architecture and Engineering Firms." *Engineering, Construction and Architectural Management* 27, no. 4 (2020): 872–92. https://doi.org/10.1108/ECAM-03-2019-0119.

Brink, Bart, and Casey Rutland. "Take BIM Processes to the Next Level with Digital Twins." BuildingSmart International, June 2020. https://www.buildingsmart.org/take-bim-processes-to-the-next-level-with-digital-twins/.

The Boundary. "Wellington Digital Twin." Wellington, New Zealand, 2021. https://www.the-boundary.com/work/wellington-digital-twin.

Buvat, Jerome, Claudia Crummenerl, Marisa Slatter, Ramya Krishna Puttur, Lucie Pasquet, and Jessine van As. "The Digital Talent Gap: Are Companies Doing Enough?" *Capgemini and LinkedIn*, 2017, 40. https://www.capgemini.com/insights/research-library/.

Camero, Andrés, and Enrique Alba. "Smart City and Information Technology: A Review." *Cities* 93 (2019): 84–94. https://doi.org/10.1016/j.cities.2019.04.014.

Chalmers University of Technology. "Digital Twin Cities Centre." A Vinnova competence centre, 2020. https://dtcc.chalmers.se/.

Chegu Badrinath, Amarnath, Yun Tsui Chang, and Shang Hsien Hsieh. "A Review of Tertiary BIM Education for Advanced Engineering Communication with Visualization." *Visualization in Engineering*, July 2016. https://doi.org/10.1186/s40327-016-0038-6.

Davey, Calayde. *"The Hatfield Digital Twin City is Approximately Twenty-Square-Kilometre Digital Development Area in South Africa (2022)."* In *Digital Twin Cities: An Instrument for Pedagogical Change*. Edited by Sadiyah Geyer: Routledge, 2024a.

Davey, Calayde. *"Coupling Foreground Digital Twin City Development Activities Directly to Background Learning Activities, Students Were Tasked to Map Formal and Informal South African Urban Areas Through OpenStreet Map (2022)."* In *Digital Twin Cities: An Instrument for Pedagogical Change*. Edited by Sadiyah Geyer. Routledge, 2024b.

Davey, Calayde. *"Foreground Education Meets Digital City Development, as Students Create Two Improved Transportation Designs in Two Days, Leveraging Their Shared Digital Intelligence (2022)."* In *Digital Twin Cities: An Instrument for Pedagogical Change*. Edited by Sadiyah Geyer. Routledge, 2024c.

Davey, Calayde. *"Exam Project Outcomes from Chemical Engineering Students Working With the Architecture Department on Urban Topics Using Digital Twin City Data for AI/ML Training (2022)."* In *Digital Twin Cities: An Instrument for Pedagogical Change*. Edited by Sadiyah Geyer. Routledge, 2024d.

Davila Delgado, Juan Manuel, and Lukumon Oyedele. "Digital Twins for the Built Environment: Learning from Conceptual and Process Models in Manufacturing." *Advanced Engineering Informatics* 49 (August 2021): 101332. https://doi.org/10.1016/j.aei.2021.101332.

Deloitte. "Africa Construction Trends Report 2020. Managing Supply Chain Risk and Disruption in Capital Projects," 2020. https://www2.deloitte.com/content/dam/Deloitte/za/Documents/energy-resources/za-Africa-Construction-Trends-2020-Final.pdf.

Department of Architecture. *The UkuDoba Method: A Methodological Framework for Effective Data Collection and Storage*. Edited by Calayde Davey. Version 3. City of Tshwane: University of Pretoria and Chalmers University of Technology, 2020.

Department of Architecture, University of Pretoria, South Africa. Postgraduate student works, 2022.

Ferré-Bigorra, Jaume, Miquel Casals, and Marta Gangolells. "The Adoption of Urban Digital Twins." *Cities* 131 (December 2022): 103905. https://doi.org/10.1016/j.cities.2022.103905.

Armstrong, Geno and Gilge, Clay "Make It, or Break It. Reimagining Governance, People and Technology in the Construction Industry: Global Construction Survey 2017." KPMG International, 2017. https://assets.kpmg/content/dam/kpmg/xx/pdf/2017/10/global-construction-survey-make-it-or-break-it.pdf.

Armstrong, Geno, Gilge Clay, and Kevin Max. "No Turning Back. An Industry Ready to Transcend: 2021 Global Construction Survey," 2021. KPMG International, 2021. https://assets.kpmg.com/content/dam/kpmg/xx/pdf/2021/08/global-construction-survey1.pdf.

Hopfstock, Anja, Michael Hovenbitzer, Florian Lindl, and Patrick Knöfel. "Building a Digital Twin for Germany. Using Large-scale, High-resolution Lidar to Support Policymakers." *GIM International*, March 2022. https://www.gim-international.com/content/article/building-a-digital-twin-for-germany.

Kane, Gerald C., Doug Palmer, Anh Nguyen Phillips, David Kiron, and Natasha Buckley. "Aligning the Organization for Its Digital Future." *MITSloan Management Review*, no. 58180 (July 2016): 1–29. https://sloanreview.mit.edu/projects/aligning-for-digital-future/.

Ketzler, Bernd, Vasilis Naserentin, Fabio Latino, Christopher Zangelidis, Liane Thuvander, and Anders Logg. "Digital Twins for Cities: A State of the Art Review." *Built Environment* 46, no. 4 (December 2020): 547–73. https://doi.org/10.2148/BENV.46.4.547.

Khodeir, Laila Mohamed, and Ashraf Ali Nessim. "Changing Skills for Architecture Students Employability: Analysis of Job Market versus Architecture Education in Egypt." *Ain Shams Engineering Journal* 11, no. 3 (2020): 811–21. https://doi.org/10.1016/j.asej.2019.11.006.

Lee, Ahyun, Kang Woo Lee, Kyong Ho Kim, and Sung Woong Shin. "A Geospatial Platform to Manage Large-scale Individual Mobility for an Urban Digital Twin Platform." *Remote Sensing* 14, no. 3 (2022): 723. https://doi.org/10.3390/rs14030723.

Mancha, Rubén, and Ganesan Shankaranarayanan. "Making a Digital Innovator: Antecedents of Innovativeness with Digital Technologies." *Information Technology and People* 34, no. 1 (2021): 318–35. https://doi.org/10.1108/ITP-12-2018-0577.

Mankowski, Robert. "City-Scale Digital Twins for Flood Resilience," February 2020. https://www.gim-international.com/content/article/city-scale-digital-twins-for-flood-resilience.

McLennan, Marsh, SK Group, and Zurich Insurance Group. *The Global Risks Report 2021. Weforum.Org*, 2021. https://www.weforum.org/reports/the-global-risks-report-2021.

Mellado, Felipe, and Eric C.W. Lou. "Building Information Modelling, Lean and Sustainability: An Integration Framework to Promote Performance Improvements in the Construction Industry." *Sustainable Cities and Society* 61 (2020): 102355. https://doi.org/10.1016/j.scs.2020.102355.

National Research Foundation. "Virtual Singapore." Government of Singapore, 2018. https://www.sla.gov.sg/articles/press-releases/2014/virtual-singapore-a-3d-city-model-platform-for-knowledge-sharing-and-community-collaboration.

Olanipekun, Ayokunle O., and Monty Sutrisna. "Facilitating Digital Transformation in Construction—A Systematic Review of the Current State of the Art." *Frontiers in Built Environment* 7 (2021): 96. https://doi.org/10.3389/fbuil.2021.660758.

Papadonikolaki, Eleni, Ilias Krystallis, and Bethan Morgan. "Digital Technologies in Built Environment Projects: Review and Future Directions." *Project Management Journal* 53, no. 5 (February 2022): 501–19. https://doi.org/10.1177/87569728211070225.

Raworth, Kate. *Doughnut Economics*. Chlesea Green Publishing, Vermont, USA, 2018.

Ribeiro, Jair. "The Digital Transformation Passes through the Digital Twins," October 2020. https://medium.com/predict/the-digital-transformation-passes-through-the-digital-twins-560804cf86d6.

Rooney, Kevin. "BIM Education. Global 2017 Update Report," May 2017. https://www.bimalliance.se/library/3041/bim_education_global_2017_update_report_v40.pdf.

Shahzad, Muhammad, Muhammad Tariq Shafiq, Dean Douglas, and Mohamad Kassem. "Digital Twins in Built Environments: An Investigation of the Characteristics, Applications, and Challenges." *Buildings* 12, no. 2 (2022): 120. https://doi.org/10.3390/buildings12020120.

Sharifi, Ayyoob, and Amir Reza Khavarian-Garmsir. "The COVID-19 Pandemic: Impacts on Cities and Major Lessons for Urban Planning, Design, and Management." *Science of the Total Environment* 749 (2020): 142391. https://doi.org/10.1016/j.scitotenv.2020.142391.

Speicher, Joe, Tracie Neuhaus, Ishita Jain, Ryan Macpherson, Jean Shia, Jess Ausinheiler, Rebecca Greenberg, and Brendan Lehan. Supporting worker success in the age of automation. (2019). https://www2.deloitte.com/content/dam/Deloitte/us/Documents/monitor-institute/us-monitor-institute-supporting-worker-success-in-the-age-of-automation.pdf.

Spitzer, Barbara, Jerome Buvat, Valerie Morel, and Subrahmanyam KVJ. "The Digital Talent Gap: Developing Skills for Today's Digital Organizations." *Capgemini Consulting and MIT The Centre for Digital Business*, 2013, 1–13. https://library.iated.org/view/SPITZER2015DIG.

Suhaili, Padil, Esa Ahmad, and Mohamed Jamal Abidah Ainah. "Soft Skills Construct for Architecture Graduate in Accordance with Industries Requirement." *International Journal of Humanities, Arts and Social Sciences* 1, no. 3 (October 2015): 119–123. https://kkgpublications.com/wp-content/uploads/2019/04/IJHSS.20002-3.pdf.

UK Construction Media. "Integrating Digital Skills in Construction," March 2022. https://www.ukconstructionmedia.co.uk/features/integrating-digital-skills-in-construction/.

UNEP. "2020 Global Status Report for Buildings and Construction." *Global Status Report*, Nairobi, 2020, 20–24. www.globalabc.org.

UN-Habitat. "World Cities Report 2020 - The Value of Sustainable Urbanization." *Sereal Untuk*, 2020. https://unhabitat.org/sites/default/files/2020/10/wcr_2020_report.pdf.

White, Gary, Anna Zink, Lara Codecá, and Siobhán Clarke. "A Digital Twin Smart City for Citizen Feedback." *Cities* 110 (2021): 103064. https://doi.org/10.1016/j.cities.2020.103064.

World Economic Forum. "The Future of Jobs Report 2020." *The Future of Jobs Report*, October 2020. https://www.weforum.org/reports/the-future-of-jobs-report-2020/.

Zhao, Fang, Olushola I. Fashola, Tolulope I. Olarewaju, and Ijeoma Onwumere. "Smart City Research: A Holistic and State-of-the-art Literature Review." *Cities* 119 (December 2021): 103406. https://doi.org/10.1016/j.cities.2021.103406.

Zukin, Sharon. "Seeing Like a City: How Tech Became Urban." *Theory and Society* 49, no. 5–6 (October 1, 2020): 941–64. https://doi.org/10.1007/s11186-020-09410-4.

3 Poorly Trained

Towards an AI Pedagogy in Architecture

Jean Jaminet, Gabriel Esquivel, and Shane Bugni

Introduction

The paradigm of drawing and its actuation by classical architectural treatise find new disciplinary relevance in current advancements in machine learning. This research examines the illustrated expositions of Italian Mannerist architect Sebastiano Serlio through the lens of artificial intelligence (AI). Parallels are identified between the representational codes established by Serlio in his drawings and the ways in which AI systems process information. Theoretical considerations are framed by the discordant pairing of analogue and digital information processing inherent to machine learning and architectural intelligence. Tools and methods are reconsidered that do not resolve in recognisable building simulations. Instead, poorly trained AI models and equivocal digital workflows resist conventional translations from drawing to building. Technological insights discovered constitute a significant disciplinary realignment regarding the discourses of language and drawing that have defined architecture since the Renaissance.

This line of inquiry is enriched with provocative visual experimentation conducted in a design seminar at Texas A&M University during the 2021 spring semester. The seminar attracted students from architecture and engineering departments, building shared intelligence from the creative and technological alliances of both disciplines. Students participated in highly mediated human-machine collaborations in which Serlio's drawings are returned to altered object status. Experimental teaching methods developed for the course involve training AI systems rather than traditional students. Within the context of a design seminar, however, traditional engagement between professors and students was equally important to the production of knowledge. Alternatively, professors guide students in conducting machine learning experiments as well as intensely speculating about and transforming computational outputs. As an explorative mode of research and teaching, results are not predetermined; instead, low-fidelity design intelligence is cultivated by corrupting the machine learning process and productively misinterpreting synthesised objects and images. Serlio's illustrated volumes initiate the following discussions about contemporary aesthetic communication and shared design agency through new modes of perception and creative digital production.

Influence of the Disciplinary Treatise

The architectural treatise is a technical-literary genre considered to be an essential part of the historical development of architecture. Sebastiano Serlio's *Tvtte l'opera d'architettvra, et prospetiva* (All the Works on Architecture and Perspective), 1619,[1] was the first treatise to include copious drawings and illustrations as a central feature of the literature, introducing a potent visual dimension to the study of architecture.[2] Serlio's imagery has initiated longstanding discussions about the entanglements between architectural language and the coded operations of orthographic projection drawing.

Architectural language is typically understood through its coded operations. Serlio was instrumental in developing this code through his canonisation of the five orders. These codes, or rules, are laid out in the earlier volumes of his treatise, then applied in the later volumes. What is fascinating about Serlio's experiments is that in applying the codes, he proceeds to vigilantly deviate from them. The results are sometimes defined by the code, where the code and the product are isomorphic—that is, a one-to-one relationship exists between the plan and the section. However, at other times, architectural elements are organised or misaligned, which suggests that a latent diagrammatic operation other than the code is at work. Serlio's understanding of architecture begins as a pictorial or analogical signal that resembles the classical buildings of Rome and Greece. This signal is subsequently scrambled by the code of the five orders and the rules of orthographic projection drawing, producing a new language that is similar to but distinct from its classical counterpart. Architectural language is not the code; the language emerges when the code is scrambled. Thus, in Serlio, we find the architectural code (transposition) entrenched within its analogical modulation (transfiguration). These insights into the discordant pairing of the analogue and the digital suggest alternative theoretical parallels between brains and computer as well as emerging modes of creative production regarding advancements in machine learning.

From Language to Code

Language cannot be separated into distinct categories—we do not have one language that is analogical (pictorial and continuous) and another that is digital (coded and discrete). According to Gilles Deleuze, "From one point of view, we think of ... analog and digital, as two completely opposite determinations. But from another point of view, we could say that every digital language and every code is deeply embedded in an analogical flux."[3] Language, therefore, is defined by the discordant pairing of both analogical and digital modes of communication. Deleuze claims that code can be utilised in three ways:

> One can make an intrinsic combination of abstract elements. One can make a combination which will yield a "message" or a "narrative", that is, which will have an isomorphic relation to a referential set. Finally, one can code the extrinsic elements in such a way that they would be reproduced in an autonomous manner by the intrinsic elements of the code (in portraits produced by a computer, for instance).[4]

These same categories are used by Deleuze in his painting seminars to parallel three types of analogy. Similar to casting a brick, the *mould is a crude or superficial analogy; resemblance is imposed from the outside*, producing a likeness to its surface. The *module* is an internal mould. Similar to a building type, which groups buildings by shared formal characteristics and functions that provide a measure against which variations are assessed, the module uses an internal logic that anticipates its potential exfoliations. *Modulation* is a "variable, temporary, and continuous" mould that produces likeness by "completely different means." Deleuze calls this third type of analogy an aesthetic analogy.[5] Deleuze's aesthetic communication theories in each of these accounts provide insight into the correspondence and interference between the analogue and the digital. A rudimentary understanding of current digital display technology may help to clarify this enigmatic concept. When digital signals are received by a display, they are continuously decoded or "unmoulded" as a field of light pulses, displayed as discrete points of colour (pixels). The signal remains coded, but the screen becomes responsive or modulates as the digital code is transplanted into the analogical flux of the pictorial image.

This modulation is where Deleuze locates the function of the diagram. "The diagram, the agent of analogical language, does not act as a code, but as a modulator."[6] The aesthetic intention of the diagram is to remove any predetermined resemblances that might be implied on the canvas or in the artist's mind. In his analysis of Francis Bacon's painting, Deleuze notes, "The manual diagram produces an irruption like a scrambled or cleaned zone, which overturns the optical coordinates as well as the tactile connection."[7] These zones distinguish Bacon's work from abstract painting (cubism) and abstract expressionism (art informel). The code is prevalent in the former—geometric shapes imply figurative resemblances (optical space of representation)—while the latter is all diagram—the modulating power of the diagram becomes inert as it is deployed across the entire canvas (tactile space of line and colour).[8] Bacon's scrambled zones, however, embody the modulating power of the diagram (Figure 3.1). Within this domain, the continual conversions between analogue and digital, figure and figuration, and optic and haptic constitute the possibility of the aesthetic act.

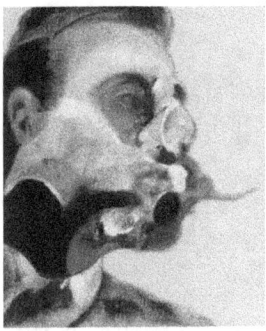 

Studies of George Dyer and Isabel Rawsthorne, 1970. Artwork © The Estate of Francis Bacon. All rights reserved, DACS/ARS/Artimage 2024. Photo: Prudence Cuming Associates Ltd.

Figure 3.1 Distorted figures in a diptych of portraits by Francis Bacon.[9] In Bacon's portrait of a male subject (left), diagrammatic interruptions appear as black colour patches that distort facial features. Bacon's depiction of a female figure (right) modulates facial features with amorphous shadows and bold brush strokes.

Significant parallels can be drawn between Deleuze's account of the diagrammatic modulation in the paintings of Francis Bacon and the analogue-to-digital conversion process performed by machine learning networks. For example, similar distorted figures can be discerned in Bacon's macabre portraits and crude AI-generated faces (Figure 3.2). In both cases, the diagram produces novel effects (or residues) and removes any predetermined resemblances that might be implied on the canvas or screen. These "scrambled or cleaned zones" are the domain of the diagram and are highly relevant to the machine learning process, particularly regarding generative adversarial networks (GANs).

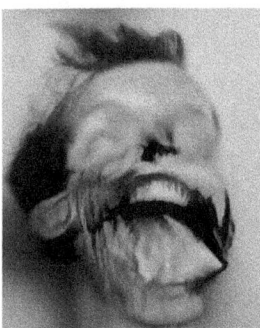 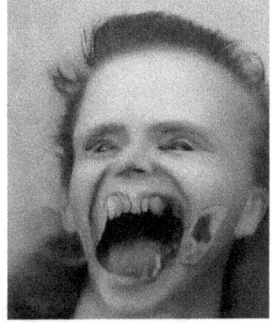

Figure 3.2 Similar "scrambled zones" visible in AI-generated faces.[10] The machine learning process produces similar "scrambled zones" that distort the facial features of a male figure (left). Similar diagrammatic interruptions are visible in an AI-generated face of a female subject resembling Bacon's portraits (right).

Poor Images

A GAN is a machine learning framework that discovers patterns from a set of training data and generates new data with the same characteristics as the training data.[11] Designers are increasingly turning to the power of GANs for image processing. The intention of these image-based GANs is to synthesise artificial images that are indistinguishable from authentic images. Every GAN has two neural networks—a generator and a discriminator. The generator synthesises new sample images from random noise, while the discriminator samples from both the initial dataset and the generator's output. The generator's output is compared to the initial dataset by the discriminator to determine whether the synthesised image can be considered real or fake. As the generator receives feedback from the discriminator, it learns to synthesise more images better resembling the input images (Figure 3.3).

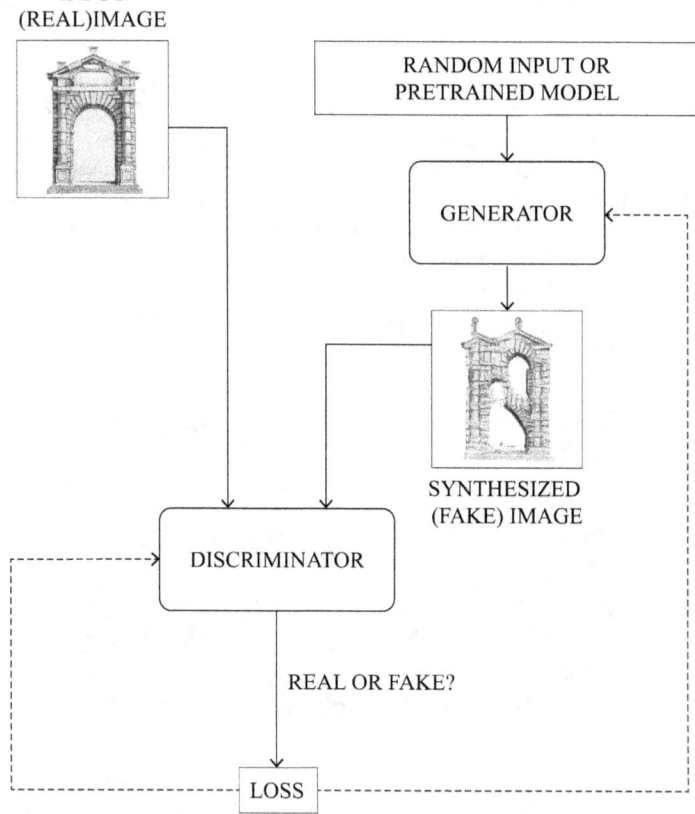

Figure 3.3 GAN architecture diagram by authors.

In this sense, diagrammatic modulation is inherent to all GANs—a continuous feedback loop transfers digital code into the analogue pictorial flow of the image in each successive training. Similar to Hito's Steyerl's "poor images" that complicate their own originality through continual digital circulation,[12] these images are equally poor. A single GAN output image is the product of synthesising multiple image inputs. Recursive computational procedures deposit layers of visual and semantic content in each successive training, eliciting a false yet perpetual agency between original and copy. When highly trained, GANs generate images that are indistinguishable from authentic images and may be easily misinterpreted as genuine data. However, their ability to deviate from initial inputs may unlock new avenues for design and creative production. The power of the GAN is not to mislead but to modulate.

Poorly Trained Models

The *poorly trained AI model* does not resolve in a highly recognisable simulation or intentionally fails to generate images that are faithful to the initial dataset. Additionally, GANs can be corrupted by introducing alternative human agency in the image training process. Flaws are introduced into the system by limiting training duration and contaminating initial datasets with foreign imagery. This process can be further complicated by layering multiple GANs. That is, the output of one GAN training can be used as the input of another, thus introducing additional feedback loops in the image generation workflow.

Moreover, poorly trained models produce *artefacts*—effects or residues made visible by their diagrammatic scrambling. Bacon might call these "involuntary free marks" and Deleuze might describe them as "*asignifying traits* that are devoid of any illustrative or narrative function."[13] These distortions and fragmentations produce alternative forms of visual intelligence that operate beyond traditional representations governed by foreground and background, light and shadow, edge and surface, and so forth. Since these conventions are not understood as such by machine learning, the poor training process synthesises objects and images that evoke alien formal, spatial, and material logic.

Towards an AI Pedagogy

A design seminar conducted during the 2021 spring semester introduced students to these urgent contemporary developments in contemporary architectural discourse.[14] Working in isolation during the COVID-19 pandemic presented opportunities to engage alternative forms of learning between professors and students. Evaluation and criticism of student design experiments were conducted through synchronous remote instruction. Virtual course delivery allowed team teaching across two universities to be more integrated as professors from both institutions could participate in bi-weekly course meetings. This mode of communication also enabled the class structure and content to be augmented with external feedback at critical points in the semester. Virtual design reviews were organised with computational intelligence experts and prominent architectural scholars from several institutions in the United States, Europe, and Asia. This type of shared intelligence enhanced subsequent machine learning experiments and expanded student perspectives with a range of critical attitudes about the bourgeoning dialogue between AI and architecture. Additionally, students' design experiments were recorded for each class meeting using a virtual whiteboard. Aside from standard file storage and sharing, this platform provided a means to collect data and review results simultaneously. The virtual whiteboard became a visual index of both successful and failed experiments. A rich and novel array of altered images, videos, and 3D objects were inscribed onto this virtual surface creating a multimedia appendix or a revised edition to Serlio's illustrated manuscripts.

The enhanced virtual laboratory became a staging ground for the exploration of advanced technological tools. Innovated methods of design intelligence were developed that involve augmenting and interpreting layered GANs that drive an integrated parametric process of three-dimensionalisation. Students were invited to participate in highly mediated human-machine collaborations in returning images of Serlio's drawings to altered object status. The intention of this experimentation was not simply to synthesise images that simulate Serlio's illustrations but rather to modulate their qualities and problematise their 2D to 3D translation beyond the rules that typically govern representations of the built environment. We discovered that high degrees of accuracy in building simulation may not be adequate in addressing the artifice of the drawing. Instead, poorly trained AI models and equivocal digital workflows produced outputs that exhibited distortions and fragmentations when reconstructing these classical artefacts from images. The poor training process was performed in three stages: (1) dataset curation, (2) layered GANs, and (3) integrated parametric three-dimensionalisation (Figure 3.4).

Dataset Curation

Image datasets collected for the seminar's AI explorations were retrieved from the Avery Architectural and Fine Arts Library's extensive online holdings of the works of Sebastiano Serlio. Avery's Digital Serlio Project[15] includes full-page digital scans of multiple published and unpublished editions of all seven of Serlio's manuscripts and several subsequently published manuscripts of collected works. To create the datasets, students downloaded manuscript pages from Avery's repository. Then, they cropped individual objects from these pages in 1024px × 1024px format to accommodate various image-based machine learning platforms.

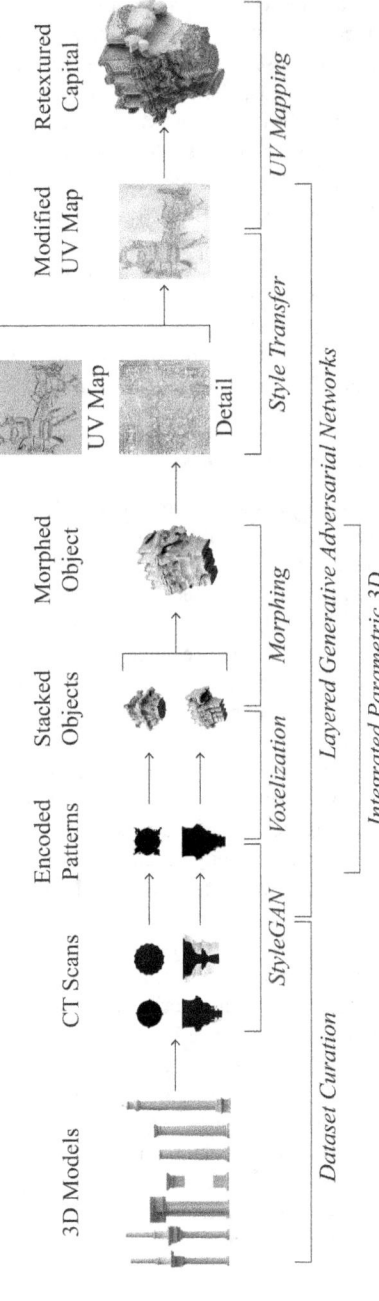

Figure 3.4 Poor training process diagram for a sample of Serlio's columns by authors.

Professors directed students to collect dataset images based on broad categories of illustrated objects—columns, porticos, plans, and facades. Although Serlio's treatise is organised based on tectonics (geometry, perspective, and orders) and typology (monuments, churches, and domestic buildings), these datasets were instead curated by object type. Since GANs require input based on superficial likeness between images, the seminar's datasets exploited the self-same repetition inherent to Serlio's drawing tectonics. These broad groupings of drawings were necessary to establish a dialogue between the coding of classical objects and the analogue-to-digital modulation of image-based neural networks. The intention of this dataset curation and subsequent 2D and 3D experimentation was to explore the capacity of the image and its qualities to suggest alternative ideas about materiality and assembly beyond the techniques of orthographic projection and its related narratives of language and representation.

Layered Generative Adversarial Networks

Following image curation, experiments were conducted by participants in the seminar to train the Serlio datasets using various GAN platforms. StyleGAN platforms require a domain of images to feed into the neural network, whereas SinGAN and style transfer models only require one or two images. Again, the primary purpose of these image-based GANs is to synthesise artificial images that maintain fidelity to the dataset. However, as a productive design tool, the seminar experiments were more interested in the latent image qualities that became evident during the training process.

In the students' initial styleGAN experiments, Serlio datasets (input images) were trained against pretrained models (generator input) by the discriminator. Instead of random noise, pretrained models—generic datasets of faces, buildings, landscapes, etc.—were preferred to expedite the training results. StyleGAN trainings predominantly generated various image distortions. Conversely, sinGAN outputs seemed to break down individual images into smaller fragments. Style transfer trainings were deployed later in the process to enhance details of subsequent 3D models.

Distortions produced reveal other shapes, profiles, and postures of the objects that move the image away from its original resemblance and semantic content. For example, a regulated facade becomes a cascading field of apertures, or a single arched opening becomes a winding surface of figural voids; both produce estrangement in silhouette and scale (Figure 3.5). These distortions are based on image values (colour, contrast, saturation, etc.) rather than formal complexity and linguistic articulation (line, edge, plane, volume, etc.). Fragmentations, on the other hand, appear as the result of separating the image into components that are detached or incomplete. For example, incongruities in patterning of a segmented masonry arch become reassembled, suggesting a tectonic that is foreign to the initial construction system. This fragmentation

Figure 3.5 StyleGAN image distortions by Brenden Bjerke (left) and Nate Gonzalez (right).

of the Serlio objects reveals alternative logics of assembly beyond the classical tectonics suggested by their orthographic projection. Of equal importance is how professors guide students through the machine learning processes by direct manipulation of the code and visual interpretation of the output.

Throughout the training processes, the degree of distortion and fragmentation can be controlled by adjusting various parameters of the GAN, including *truncation value* and *scale of manipulation*. The adjustment of these parameters allows designers to claim agency in the machine learning process to control the fidelity to the initial input datasets and the uniqueness of the output. The intention of these methods was not to synthesise columns, facades, or doorways that would be indistinguishable from Serlio's illustrations but to use the digital code of the GAN as a substitute for the architectural or orthographic code to scramble the analogue pictorial signal of the image.

Integrated Parametric Three-dimensionalisation

Industry-standard 3D modelling software platforms use mathematical coordinate-based representations to simulate surface and mesh geometry. These models begin as primitive shapes (curve, cube, sphere, etc.) that gain complexity by augmenting the component geometry. Geometry is manually created and manipulated through direct access to its points, curves, surfaces, and polygons displayed as orthographic projection drawings in multiple default windows of the user interface. These platforms give designers the power to create any 3D object by drawing on skills of visual and tactile acuity and knowledge of conventional representational systems.

Other 3D modelling and animation software applications utilise procedural generation tools rather than coordinate-based geometry. *Procedural generation* "is a method of generating data or content algorithmically as opposed to manually that combines human-generated assets and algorithms with computer-generated randomness and processing power."[16] The gaming industry uses procedural generation tools to generate environments in realtime, providing an immersive experience of limitless variation based on choices made by the player. Likewise, they are used in movie editing to create fantasy landscapes and crowd swarms with unprecedented randomness.[17] These tools limit direct access to the 3D model; instead, design agency is asserted by adjusting the parametric constraints available in the code.

In student experiments, procedural generation tools created 3D geometry directly from GAN outputs through *voxelisation* of the image content. Voxelisation uses digital colour values to create 3D geometry from 2D image data. Every digital image is composed of a rectangular array of colours; each unit in this grid is called a pixel. The image is three-dimensionalised by converting the 2D squares in a pixel grid into 3D cubes called voxels or volumetric pixels. This 3D grid of cubes is augmented by assigning various depth values to the spectrum of colours in the image, which produces a wide range of 3D shapes, profiles, and textures. Students also used a process called *voxel stacking*, which generates 3D geometry from a series of layered images (Figure 3.6). In this process, voxels are generated from individual images and interpolated between images, thereby creating more complex spatial geometry. The number of and spacing between images are additional variables that can be adjusted to modify the 3D results.

Seminar participants also used coordinate-based 3D modelling to generate generic geometry and render various 3D outputs. These standard modelling applications further enabled student design researchers to visualise and augment GAN outputs as material textures through ultraviolet (UV) *mapping* (Figure 3.6). UV mapping is a virtual process by which 3D geometry of a

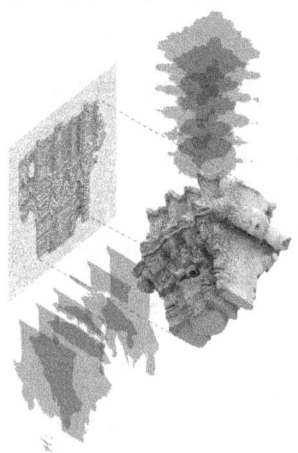

Figure 3.6 Representation of voxel stacking and ultraviolet (UV) mapping by John Scott.

Poorly Trained 67

digital model is unfolded as a flat surface to which 2D images and graphics can be placed or "mapped" and edited.[18] "U" and "V" denote the coordinate axes of the 2D surface, where as "X" and "Y" represent these coordinates on the 3D geometry of a digital model. This mathematical representation allows the modified 2D surface to be refolded onto the 3D model with high degrees of precision. To accompany this description of the poor training process, three student-conducted experiments from the seminar are outlined below that illustrate various human-machine collaborations in further detail.

Operative Model: Column

Serlio's orthographic representations of columns are the subject of this student-conducted AI experiment to discover new patterns of formal articulation and latent assembly logics within classical tectonic systems. First, several coordinate-based 3D models were constructed from various drawings of Serlio's columns. These 3D models were analysed and reinterpreted as a series of horizontal and vertical cross-sections. These continuous cross-sections were envisioned as computer tomographic (CT) scans rather than conventional plans and sections cut at specific heights and depths. Corresponding horizontal and vertical cross-sections were trained separately on styleGAN to synthesise new hybridised profile shapes (Figure 3.7). These new *encoded patterns* were used as the inputs for subsequent processes of three-dimensionalisation and assembly.

The encoded patterns were stacked using procedural generation tools to voxelise the graphic content by assigning depth values to their range of black-and-white pixels—black pixels create positive 3D mass. Corresponding horizontal and vertical stacked models (Figure 3.8) were morphed to create a hybrid object exhibiting both sectional and planimetric characteristics. The

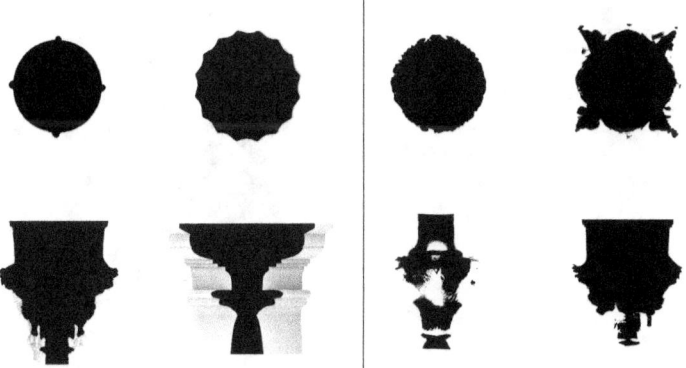

Figure 3.7 CT scans (left) and encoded patterns (right) by John Scott.

Figure 3.8 Models created through voxel stacking by John Scott (left) and Luis Sanabria (right).

striated, crystalline, or fractal qualities of these stacked and hybridised 3D models are a result of augmenting and interpolating voxel matter and further amplify the recursive nature of machine learning. An alternative assembly logic emerges that is a matter of data processing rather than tectonic joinery or orthographic projection.

Surface articulation of the morphed object was further complicated by a neural style transfer that blends the characteristics of two input images. The first input was the morphed object's UV map—a 2D image representing the unfolded geometry of a 3D model. The second input was a selected Serlio's detail image. The morphed object was then rewrapped with the style transfer output image (Figure 3.9). Once reintegrated, the augmented map displaces the surface of the morphed object, creating textural misalignments that are apparent by the presence of empty patches or bald spots. These surface effects suggest new kinds of ornaments that are alien to the architectural orders and deviate in varying degrees from the surface geometry of the column.

Figure 3.9 Style transfer output (left) and rewrapped morphed object (right) by John Scott.

Operative Model: Portico

One of Serlio's major contributions to architectural discourse is his canonisation of the classical orders. These architectural components (columns, arches, pediments, etc.) are exhibited and analysed as fragments in his early volumes, then deployed in larger building configurations. Nowhere in his treatise is this mereology more evident than in the *Extraordinario Libro*[19] that illustrates prototype doorways (porticos) in which these components are deployed and combined with unprecedented variation. Students speculated about these part-to-whole relationships using Serlio's portico images as the raw material for the following AI experiment.

This operative model utilises various GANs in the image training process to estrange the image content. First, a curated dataset of portico images was processed by a styleGAN, the output of which inherits multiple features of individual porticos. Due to the similarity between input images, the most productive synthesised images exhibit distortions of the architectural components (details), while the overall figures (silhouettes) remain largely unchanged. Based on these characteristics, a single output image was selected as the input for a succeeding sinGAN training. The intention of introducing the sinGAN was to fragment the portico image into multiple parts (Figure 3.10).

A sinGAN selects patches of elements it can recognise and repeat to create "diverse samples that carry the same visual content as the [input] image."[20] This process can be useful in generating images that simulate the randomness in natural environments, cityscapes, flocks, and swarms. However, when trained on an image that depicts a singular object, the sinGAN produces unexpected configurations that have the effect of fragmenting rather than unifying the image. The resulting fragmented portico images create alternative components loosely based on the textures of the illustration.

The subsequent 3D assembly process combines both procedural generation tools and conventional 3D modelling. Individual output images were voxelised by assigning depth values to their range of black-and-white pixels. Two of the resulting voxelised components were morphed to produce an object that inherits 3D information from both. This merged object was then combined with a 3D model of a recognisable portico element (Figure 3.11). A

Figure 3.10 StyleGAN distortion (left) and sinGAN fragmentation (right) by Spencer Young.

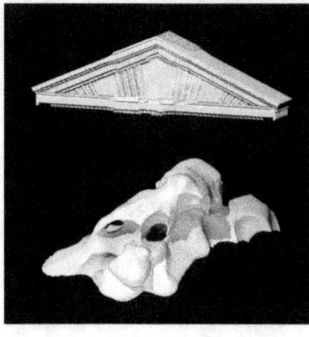 

Figure 3.11 High- and low-fidelity components (left) form an eroded artefact (right) by Spencer Young.

novel hybrid artefact is contrived that simultaneously exhibits the figuration of voxelised components (scrambled digital code) and partial reconstruction of the familiar language of architecture (pictorial analogue signal). Furthermore, this highly mediated process of three-dimensionalisation creates an erosion effect that obscures these formal and visual relationships.

The final tactic in this operative model deploys a neural style transfer to explore other ideas about surface detail. Similar to the column model, the hybrid artefact's UV map was blended with a Serlio's detail image. These articulations do not reveal the nature of materials or the process of assembly. Instead, they appear as hieroglyphics etched onto a vermiculated form (Figure 3.12). Students discovered a remnant of an alien manuscript or the spolia from a fallen civilisation inscribed onto, which is an enigmatic language yet to be deciphered. This archaeological process of estrangement, 3D assembly, and stylisation discloses

 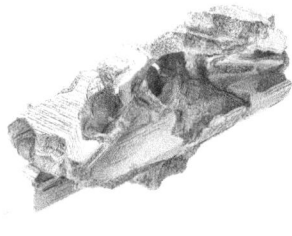

Figure 3.12 Style transfer output (left) and rewrapped vermiculated form (right) by Spencer Young.

an alternative architectural narrative shaped by image and data enhancement rather than the tectonics of orthography.

Operative Model: Façade

A building's facade is its primary interface between the inside and the outside. The apparent congruence of this relationship has been the subject of much speculation throughout the history of architecture. For example, Leon Batista Alberti's rigorously composed Renaissance facade of the "Palazzo Rucellai"[21] conceals an irregular accumulation of existing structures, rooms, and courtyards within. Likewise, Serlio's "Dwelling for a King"[22] hides a labyrinth of disparate rooms behind its highly disciplined facade. Students reinterpreted Serlio's anomalous interface between exterior surface and interior space in the following machine learning experiment.

First, curated datasets of Serlio's façades were processed by a styleGAN. During the training process, students adjusted the GAN's parameters, including truncation value and scale of manipulation, to control how much image distortion and fragmentation occurred. Lower truncation values synthesised images that were more self-similar to the initial dataset, whereas higher values produced results that deviated significantly. Likewise, increasing the scale of manipulation created highly articulated images (changes the detail but not the figure of the image), decreasing this value created chunky or fragmented images (reduces detail but amplifies figuration). Access to these parameters allows students to claim agency in the machine learning process by modulating the fidelity to the initial input datasets and the uniqueness of the output.

As in previous experiments, synthesised façade images were converted into black-and-white patterns from which preliminary 3D models were generated through voxel stacking. This procedure presented an initial challenge involving the representation of windows. As an orthographic drawing, Serlio's fenestrations are rendered with black fill and appear as geometric voids within the surface of the façade. However, as a digital image, the opposite effect is produced—black registers as solid and white registers as void. To exploit this ambiguity between figure and ground, students created separate stacked objects in which windows register as solid in some instances and void in others (Figure 3.13).

A second and more pervasive challenge involved amplifying the latent spatial qualities within the flat façade illustrations. Because of the highly recognisable and geometrically regulated nature of these representations, students found difficulty using similar workflows to estrange this image content. Instead, they reevaluated their methodology and adjusted the parameters of the experiment to overcome limitations of their preliminary model. Additional tactics were invented and deployed to augment the compressed spatial dimension of the façade images. In this case, a second procedural generation

Figure 3.13 Encoded pattern (left) and voxel-stacked object with solid windows (right) by Erin Carter.

technique was used to scatter the initial stacked object into multiple parts. This decomposition technique used other scripted combinations of colour values when voxelising the image content, thereby decoding embedded representational information. The façade is no longer an envelope that delimits space but rather a vessel that contains hidden cavities and figural voids that simultaneously reshape its boundaries (Figure 3.14).

A similar style transfer and UV mapping strategy was introduced to further amplify relationships between surface and opening. Once reintegrated, the hyper-articulated decoration disregards surface tectonics and appears as esoteric glyphs foreign to the language of architecture. The resulting morphological assembly deviates significantly from conventional surface fenestration and exhibits novel solid-void relationships which are window no less than room (Figure 3.15).

Figure 3.14 Models created through voxel stacking (left) and decomposition technique (right) by Erin Carter.

Poorly Trained 73

Figure 3.15 Morphological assembly (right) with hyper-articulated decoration that appears as esoteric glyphs (left) by Austin White.

Conclusions

The paradigm of drawing has undergone radical change due to the demands of virtual design production and no longer provides a stable reference for the discipline of architecture. "Images are inherently dynamic, and our tendency to think of them as static or fixed is a result of the psycho-historical residue of drawings ...."[23] Furthermore, the facility with which these images can be manipulated suggests that the drawing no longer constitutes an original act of creation. Serlio anticipated these contemporary technological circumstances by creating his own dataset 400 years before IBM coined the term. Likewise, the transformation of these drawings into printed images in the sixteenth century and scanned images in the twenty-first century further complicates their authenticity. The ever-present problem of agency within the discipline necessitates a revisitation of these manuals through a hyper-digital lens.

Beyond intentions to reinterpret historical artefacts and deploy novel design technologies, the focus of this experimental pedagogy is to address the transformative potential of AI in architecture. AI is not simply a toolset to optimise building elements but rather emphasises architecture's ability to serve as a cultural marker. Mario Carpo observes that in failing to recognise opportunities to expand architectural intelligence through technology, "the design professions seem to have flatly rejected a techno-cultural development that would weaken (or, in fact, recast) some of their traditional authorial privileges."[24] These assertions radically challenge computational methodologies as tools of expediency and efficiency and, more importantly, embrace the possibility of using them as strategies of communication between the human mindset and alien intelligence.

By surrendering established roles of authorship, the experimental methodologies presented here introduce alternative design agency in the machine learning process through visual selection and interpretation, thus fostering a shared ownership between designer and machine. The machine is tasked with indiscriminately processing content through iteration, replication, and complication of data through feedback loops in the computational process. As such, human intervention is required at the level of mundane digital tasks and post-processing image manipulation. As Abrons and Fure note, "Designers can take up this challenge by critically considering the digital processes we take for granted, such as default render settings, photoshop filters, geometric primitives, 'pan' and 'zoom,' extrude commands, and so forth."[25] These discerning manoeuvres can be further integrated to varying degrees at different stages rather than coming at the end of a more linear design process. Seemingly trivial operations become the primary form of mediation between human perception and machine learning.

Remote learning has increased the design disciplines' reliance on digital media, especially in shaping the built environment. In our seminar, provocative digital production proliferates from shared design intelligence and innovative modes of virtual communication between professors, students, and machines. However, substituting physical learning spaces for various screen-based modalities has seemingly intensified distinctions between the analogue and the digital. As we emerge from the COVID-19 pandemic, these measures draw attention to the need for equally novel physical experimentation. Integrating physical production into the poor training process was an initial goal of the seminar, and several student experiments resulted in digitally fabricated artefacts. However, restricted access to essential infrastructure limited concentrated experimentation to the virtual environment. Without the critical oversight and rigour that continue to reside within the domain of the design studio, these physical objects merely simulated their virtual counterparts in extruded plastic filament. Like celebrities who modify their physical appearance to make their image more adaptable to social media, other models of physical building simulation are likewise complicated by digital media interference. We speculate that the hyper-mediated status of the drawing requires additional experimentation to uncover the translational consequences when moving from altered image to physical artefact.

What we learned from these experiments is that the poorly trained image-to-object workflow contests the hegemony of drawing tectonics and assembly logics associated with orthography. These human-machine collaborations rework the way we present, learn, and teach architecture because they scramble the orthographic codes or conventions that have defined architectural language since the Renaissance and have persisted through pedagogies established by the École des Beaux-Arts and the Bauhaus. Our pedagogical model focused on student-conducted experiments serves as conduits to initiate discussions about contemporary aesthetic communication and shared design agency that provide future architects with a unique disciplinary perspective on our technological circumstances. Machine learning of this kind signals a shift away from modern and postmodern notions of consistency, semantics, and representation toward a new paradigm of medium, communication, and agency. The examination of

Serlio's illustrated volumes through the lens of AI stimulates alternative modes of perception and creative digital production, alluding to new languages and forms of expression yet to be discovered.

Notes

1 Sebastiano Serlio, *Tvtte L'opera D'architettvra, et Prospetiva*, ed. Giovanni Domenico Scamozzi, Di Nuouo Ristampate, and con Ogni Diligenza Corrette, repr. with annotations by John Webb (1619; repr., Ridgewood, NJ: The Gregg Press Incorporated, 1964).
2 Francesco Benelli, "The Life and Work of Sebastiano Serlio," Digital Serlio Project, Avery Architectural & Fine Arts Library (2018), March 15, 2021, https://library.columbia.edu/libraries/avery/digitalserlio/essays/benelli.html.
3 Gilles Deleuze, "Painting and the Question of Concepts/05," trans. Billy Dean Goehring, The Deleuze Seminars (1981), March 14, 2021, https://deleuze.cla.purdue.edu/lecture/lecture-05-4/.
4 Gilles Deleuze, *Francis Bacon: The Logic of Sensation*, trans. Daniel W. Smith (New York: Continuum, 2003), 114.
5 Deleuze, "Painting."
6 Deleuze, *Francis Bacon*, 120.
7 Ibid., 137.
8 Ibid., 104.
9 Francis Bacon, *Studies of George Dyer and Isabel Rawsthorne*, 1970, diptych, oil on canvas, each panel 14 × 12 in. (35.5 × 30.5 cm).
10 Mario Klingemann, *StyleGAN2: Mapping Music to Facial Expression in Real Time*, Video, YouTube, May 29, 2022, https://www.youtube.com/watch?v=A6bo_mIOto0.
11 John Brockman, ed., *Possible Minds: 25 Ways of Looking at AI* (New York: Penguin Press, 2019), 224–226.
12 Hito Steyerl, "In Defense of the Poor Image," E-flux Journal, no. 10 (2009), March 14, 2021, https://www.e-flux.com/journal/10/61362/in-defense-of-the-poor-image/.
13 Deleuze, *Francis Bacon*, 5.
14 All design research was conducted during the 2021 spring semester at Texas A&M University College of Architecture under the instruction of Jean Jaminet and Gabriel Esquivel and with the assistance of Shane Bugni. Student contributors include Brenden Bjerke, Erin Carter, Emily Cuevas, Nate Gonzalez, Kamryn Massey, Ana Rico Rubio, John Scott, Dalton Turpin, Spenser Young, Austin White, and Luis Sanabria.
15 Avery Architectural and Fine Arts Library, "Digital Serlio Project," Columbia University Libraries (2018), March 15, 2021, https://library.columbia.edu/libraries/avery/digitalserlio.html.
16 Wikipedia, s.v., "Procedural Generation," last modified May 18, 2022, 13:53, https://en.wikipedia.org/wiki/Procedural_generation.
17 Shivang Sarawagi, "Procedural Generation—A Comprehensive Guide Put in Simple Words," Scaleyourapp (2021), May 19, 2022, https://www.scaleyourapp.com/procedural-generation-a-comprehensive-guide-in-simple-words/.
18 Hans Tursak, "Theoretical Notes on the Aesthetics of Architectural Texture Mapping," in *Distributed Proximities: Volume 1*, ed. Brian Slocum et al. (Delaware: Acadia Publishing Company, 2021), 678.
19 *Sebastiano Serlio on Architecture*, trans. Vaughan Hart and Peter Hicks, vol. 2, *Books VI-VII of "Tutte l'opere d'architettura et prospetiva" with "Castrametation of the Romans" and "The Extraordinary Book of Doors"* (New Haven: Yale University Press, 2001).

20 Ramar Rott Shaham, Tali Dekel, and Romer Michaeli, "SinGAN: Learning a Generative Model from a Single Natural Image," https://arxiv.org/pdf/1905.01164.pdf (2019).
21 Leon Battista Alberti, "Pallazo Rucellai," Florence, Italy, 1446–1451.
22 Sebastiano Serlio, *Serlio Book VI Plate 46*-47, circa 1550, Architectural drawing, Columbia Digital Library Collections, New York, https://doi.org/10.7916/D87W7VX8.
23 John May, *Signal, Image, Architecture* (New York: Columbia University Press, 2019), 47.
24 Mario Carpo, *The Second Digital Turn: Design Beyond Intelligence* (Cambridge: MIT Press, 2017), 5.
25 Ellie Abrons and Adam Fure. "Post-Digital Materiality," in *Lineament: Material, Representation and the Physical Figure in Architectural Production*, eds. GP Borden and Michael Meredith (New York: Routledge, 2017), 187.

Bibliography

Avery Architectural and Fine Arts Library. "Digital Serlio Project," Columbia University Libraries (2018), March 15, 2021, https://library.columbia.edu/libraries/avery/digitalserlio.html.
Benelli, Francesco. "The Life and Work of Sebastiano Serlio." Digital Serlio Project, Avery Architectural & Fine Arts Library (2018), March 15, 2021, https://library.columbia.edu/libraries/avery/digitalserlio/essays/benelli.html.
Bostrom, Nick. *Superintelligence: Paths, Dangers, Strategies*. Oxford: Oxford University Press, 2017.
Brockman, John, ed. *Possible Minds: 25 Ways of Looking at AI*. New York: Penguin Press, 2019.
Carpo, Mario. *Architecture in the Age of Printing: Orality, Writing, Typography, and Printed Images in the History of Architectural Theory*. Translated by Sarah Benson. Cambridge: MIT Press, 2001.
Carpo, Mario. *The Second Digital Turn: Design Beyond Intelligence*. Cambridge: MIT Press, 2017.
Deleuze, Gilles. *Francis Bacon: The Logic of Sensation*. Translated by Daniel W. Smith. New York: Continuum, 2003.
Deleuze, Gilles. "Painting and the Question of Concepts/05." The Deleuze Seminars (1981), March 14, 2021, https://deleuze.cla.purdue.edu/seminars/painting-and-question-concepts/lecture-05.
May, John. *Signal, Image, Architecture*. New York: Columbia University Press, 2019.
Pollio, Marcus Vitruvius. *The Ten Books on Architecture*. Translated by Morgan M. Hicky. New York: Dover, 1960.
Sarawagi, Shivang. "Procedural Generation—A Comprehensive Guide Put in Simple Words." Scaleyourapp (2021), May 19, 2022, https://www.scaleyourapp.com/procedural-generation-a-comprehensive-guide-in-simple-words/.
Serlio, Sebastiano. *Sebastiano Serlio on Architecture*. Vol. 2, *Books VI-VII of "Tutte l'opere d'architettura et prospetiva"* with *"Castrametation of the Romans"* and *"The Extraordinary Book of Doors,"* translated by Vaughan Hart and Peter Hicks. New Haven: Yale University Press, 2001.
Serlio, Sebastiano. *Tvtte L'opera D'architettvra, et Prospetiva*, edited by Giovanni Domenico Scamozzi, Di Nuouo Ristampate, and con Ogni Diligenza Corrette edition,

1619. Reprinted with annotations by John Webb. Ridgewood, NJ: The Gregg Press Incorporated, 1964.

Shaham, Tamar Rott, Tali Dekel, and Tomer Michaeli. "SinGAN: Learning a Generative Model from a Single Natural Image." https://arxiv.org/pdf/1905.01164.pdf (2019).

Shores, Corry. "Deleuze's Analog and Digital Communication." Pirates and Revolutionaries (2009), March 14, 2021, http://piratesandrevolutionaries.blogspot.com/2009/01/deleuzes-analog-and-digital.html.

Steyerl, Hito. "In Defense of the Poor Image." E-flux Journal, no. 10 (2009), https://www.e-flux.com/journal/10/61362/in-defense-of-the-poor-image/.

Tursak, Hans. "Theoretical Notes on the Aesthetics of Architectural Texture Mapping." In *Distributed Proximities: Volume 1*, edited by Brian Slocum, Viola Ago, Shelby Doyle, Adam Marcus, Maria Yablonina, and Matias del Campo, 678–687. Delaware: Acadia Publishing Company, 2021.

4 A Point Cloud Pedagogy

Robert Stepnoski

Summary

In the last decade, point cloud datasets, created using various technologies, have revolutionised the way we document in three dimensions. It has had a massive impact on many fields, among them those of relevance to this chapter: architectural history and conservation. Within this context, this chapter discusses what it defines as "A Point Cloud Pedagogy": a teaching methodology aimed at providing students with new insight into Historic Preservation using point cloud technology, photogrammetry, and 3D laser scanning methods as the vehicle. Photogrammetry and 3D laser scanning methods of documentation are not necessarily new; however, improvements in the technology have made this far more accessible to students in recent years. The thesis behind this teaching methodology is that a better understanding of how to grasp, process, and draw conclusions using these increasingly accessible tools will allow students to discover what it takes to document a historic site more fully.

This chapter will argue that the story of a historic site can best be told at varying scales and levels of detail within the point cloud itself. This, it will suggest, offers the opportunity to analyse each part of the site and visualise the 3D model through point cloud, wireframe, shaded, and rendered views. In addition, we argue that 3D laser scans and photogrammetry allow the user to develop a free-standing model of underground interior spaces,[1] which would otherwise not be seen. This can provide a whole new insight into a historic site and provide clues as to what might be missing and what might need to be further investigated. Understanding the blend of sciences, art, and precision of measurement involved in advanced photogrammetry and 3D laser scanning methods provides students with new perspectives, forcing them to wonder what they are viewing, what story lies behind the resultant image, and how they may approach it. In discussing these advances in recent architectural conservation practices and teaching then, this chapter opens debates about the latest tendencies and possible educational benefits of 3D laser scans and photogrammetry in ways that are far more significant than just the technologies involved.

DOI: 10.4324/9781003435396-5

Introduction

Each student has taken a unique approach with documenting their own independent field studies using advanced photogrammetry technologies. This includes a range of capture devices, including the latest smart phones, point and shoot cameras, DSLRs (Digital Single-Lens Reflex), and UAVs (Unmanned Aerial Vehicle). Students in this "Realty Capture for Architecture" class learned to document using a new medium while applied to varying scales of architectural detail and landscapes.[2] Each approach offered a new method of analysis and representation of the 3D point cloud digital assets. This offered students the means to measure and refine their point cloud models for the highest level of accuracy possible. Application of this technology into the teaching workflows, with point clouds captured, acquired by students and the professor, provided a departure from the classic form of teaching and drawing. This offered the opportunity to use the point cloud as the vehicle or tool to generate an accurate documentation of the historic site. This would be used to inform the story of the site told by the student and support their conclusions. "Realty Capture for Architecture" is a course given at the University of Texas at Austin, School of Architecture,[3] ideally suited for any students interested in tying together 3D scanning techniques with virtual reality models. The class is set to compare and contrast capture technologies appropriate for a variety of site and environmental conditions. It provides a broad understanding of how to take raw data from a site, turn it into useful models, apply specific techniques to enhance the models, and how the processes can be used in diverse fields of study or work.

Digital Heritage Preservation,[4] historic sites, their point clouds, and point cloud datasets were provided to the students as a parallel learning opportunity, each supporting the other. This brought a real-world aspect of how and when to use point cloud technologies, reinforcing the technical skillset each student would work to improve upon during the course. This chapter focuses on the learning components used to build each student's skillset and learn to see a historic site from a very different approach. The added benefit of generating and working with the point cloud datasets was extraordinary images that would have previously been impossible to create. Each student learned to present with layered point clouds, vignettes, and display of subterranean or hidden spaces with the point cloud. The combination of different elements, such as mesh (which is a network of lines and shapes that form the basis of a 3D model), wireframe (a skeletal model showing the basic structure), 3D textured mesh (a detailed 3D model with textures), and individual points, resulted in creating a visually striking and powerful image.

Digital Heritage Preservation

Combining the study and exploration of historic sites with the creation of digital 3D point cloud models provided the students with a unique and engaging learning experience. By working with real-world sites and data, the students were able to see how their work in the digital realm translated to the physical world. The use of historic sites also provided a rich context for learning about the cultural and historical significance of each site as well as the challenges and opportunities presented by working with older structures and materials. This hybrid approach allowed the students to develop a deep understanding of both the technical and cultural aspects of digital 3D point cloud modelling.

The hands-on nature of the project allowed the students to develop critical thinking and problem-solving skills as they navigated the various challenges and complexities of working with photogrammetry and 3D scanning technologies. By engaging with the material in a meaningful way, the students were able to develop a deep and lasting understanding of the subject matter.

Overall, the hybrid learning experience provided by this project was a powerful tool for engaging students and helping them to develop the skills and knowledge needed to work with digital 3D point cloud models. By combining technical training with real-world exploration and analysis, the students were able to develop a deep and lasting understanding of this exciting and rapidly evolving field. Selecting a diverse range of sites from around the world and locally, the students were able to apply their digital workflows in a variety of contexts and settings. This allowed them to gain a broad understanding of how these technologies can be applied across different cultures and architectural styles.

For example, working with sites in different locations provided the students with the opportunity to explore different lighting conditions and weather patterns, which can have a significant impact on the quality of the data captured through photogrammetry and 3D scanning.[5] They were able to learn how to adjust their workflows and techniques to accommodate for these differences, ensuring that they were able to capture accurate and detailed data regardless of the site's location. Working with sites of different architectural styles allowed the students to explore the unique challenges and opportunities presented by each type of structure. For example, they were able to learn how to capture the intricate details of ornate historical buildings as well as the clean lines and minimalist designs of modern architecture. The use of a diverse range of sites helped the students to develop a more nuanced and adaptable approach to their digital workflows. By learning how to apply these techniques across different contexts and settings, they were able to develop a deeper understanding of the possibilities and limitations of these technologies.

A heritage is something that is, or should be, passed from generation to generation because it is valued.[6] Exploring a select list of historic point clouds around Austin, TX, and a look at a few projects and the approach of CyArk provided the students with their first dive into historic sites. This provided a better understanding of the digital documentation approach taken to capture the site as a snapshot in time. United Nations Educational, Scientific and Cultural Organization (UNESCO) World Heritage sites such as Sydney Opera House, Sydney, Australia,[7] Meuse-Argonne American Cemetery

A Point Cloud Pedagogy 81

Romagne-sous-Montfaucon, France,[8] Monastery of Geghard, Armenia,[9] excavations and airborne mapping at Aguada Fénix, Mexico,[10] were explored and studied in depth to understand the methods and workflows used and why we use them. Local sites such as Mueller Control Tower, Austin, TX,[11] Littlefield Carriage House, Austin, TX,[12] and the Seaholm Power Plant Intake Building, Austin, TX,[13] provided the anchor needed for the students to see firsthand what workflows were used on historic sites they would be able to visit in person.

Independent Field Study

Using the tools on hand, the students were able to make key decisions throughout the process to ensure that the full story of the site was captured. This may have involved decisions about camera placement, lighting conditions, and data processing techniques, among other things. By carefully considering these factors and making informed decisions, the students were able to produce a comprehensive and accurate record of the historic site. This demonstrates the importance of using a thoughtful and deliberate approach when documenting historic buildings as well as the value of having access to high-quality tools and technology. By learning these skills, the students can apply them to future projects and contribute to the preservation and documentation of important cultural heritage sites.

The students took a comprehensive approach to capturing the material, texture, and spatial qualities of the historic sites they documented. This involved carefully selecting scan locations and implementing UAV flights to capture both interior and exterior spaces. By using high-quality imaging equipment and sophisticated data processing techniques, the students were able to produce detailed records of the material and texture of the building surfaces as well as the layout and configuration of interior spaces. This approach is important for several reasons. First, by documenting the material and texture of the building surfaces, the students were able to capture important details about the building's construction and history. This information can be used to inform future restoration and preservation efforts. Second, by documenting the layout and configuration of interior spaces, the students were able to gain a deeper understanding of how the building was used and experienced by its occupants. This information can be used to inform future research and interpretation efforts. Overall, the students' focus on material, texture, and spatial qualities demonstrates the importance of taking a comprehensive approach to documenting historic sites. By capturing multiple dimensions of the building's physical and experiential qualities, the students were able to produce a more complete record of the building and its history.

Additional Light Detection and Ranging (LiDAR) scans and Unmanned Aerial Vehicle (UAV) flights to gather a higher level of detail in the point cloud data is an important consideration when documenting historic sites, as it can be difficult to capture every detail with a single scan or flight. By performing additional scans or flights, the students were able to increase the overall detail of the final densified point cloud. This approach can be particularly helpful when capturing small or intricate details, such as ornate carvings or intricate mouldings. By capturing these details at multiple angles or altitudes, the students were able to produce a more complete record of the building's physical features. While additional scans and flights can be helpful for capturing more detail, they can also increase the complexity of the data processing workflow. It's important to carefully manage and organise the data to ensure that it can be easily integrated into a final point cloud model. With careful planning and execution, however, additional scans and flights can be a valuable tool for capturing the full story of a historic site.

What was discovered upon the first site visits were a few dozen images that were not enough to document their chosen buildings or historic sites. Depending on the size and complexity of the site, it can require hundreds or even thousands of images to produce a detailed point cloud model. This highlights the importance of careful planning and preparation when embarking on a photogrammetry or 3D scanning project. It's important to thoroughly assess the site and determine the optimal number and placement of images or scans needed to produce an accurate and comprehensive model. In some cases, additional site visits or data collection efforts may be necessary to capture the full scope of the site. This may involve taking more images, performing additional scans or UAV flights, or using alternative data collection methods such as LiDAR.[14] Ultimately, the goal of any photogrammetry or 3D scanning project should be to produce a detailed and accurate record of the site that can be used for research, preservation, and education purposes. By carefully planning and executing the data collection process, the students were able to produce high-quality point cloud models that provided a wealth of insights into their chosen historic sites.

By processing their first datasets, the students were able to identify areas where additional data collection was necessary to fill in gaps or improve the quality of the point cloud model. This may have included taking more images or performing additional scans or UAV flights. One advantage of photogrammetry and 3D scanning technologies is their ability to capture data quickly and efficiently, which allows for multiple site visits to be completed in a relatively short amount of time. This makes it possible to iteratively refine the point cloud model as needed to produce a high-quality final product. Overall, the students' experience underscores the importance of careful planning and ongoing evaluation throughout the data collection process. By being responsive to the needs of the site and adapting their approach as necessary, the students were able to produce detailed and accurate point cloud models that captured the full story of each historic site. Hundreds of images turned into several thousand images to provide adequate overlap and detail coverage of their sites to allow the story to be told.

Finding Detail

What happened during this process for all students was a new appreciation for how that building touched the ground. Looking at a building beyond its façade involves examining its different elements and paying attention to details that are often overlooked. This can involve exploring the corners, fenestrations (windows and doors), eaves (the projecting edge of a roof), and other hidden details and features. This type of examination can provide a deeper understanding of the building's design, history, and purpose. By taking a closer look at these elements, one can appreciate the building's character and unique qualities, which are often not immediately visible. This can be especially important for historic buildings, as these elements can provide valuable insight into the architectural styles and construction techniques of the past.

Once that level of attention to detail is found, how to capture it using photogrammetry became the challenge. Colour, texture, and light (preferably even or diffuse light)[15] were goals to reflect in the 3D point cloud models. Each historic site chosen by the students held a very different set of challenges in capture.

Acquiring the range of textures and materials, such as rough stone with deep reveals and smooth homogenous white stucco, into a point cloud can present a challenge in photogrammetry. This is because different textures and materials can affect the way that light is reflected, which can impact the accuracy of the photogrammetry process. However, by discovering the different conditions and taking steps to account for them, the students were able to produce accurate and detailed point clouds. This shows the importance of carefully considering the materials and textures when using photogrammetry, as they can significantly impact the final result. By overcoming this challenge, the students were able to gain a deeper understanding of photogrammetry and the importance of considering the conditions of the subject being captured.

In the case of capturing an entire building façade with ornate features, doorway entry points, an expanse of art across a brick wall, or turns in the wall itself, students made choices as to where to capture more details of the subject they are capturing.[16] What detail would provide more content to support the story of this subject? Layers or loops are necessary when performing the photogrammetry workflows, stepping back twenty, sometimes, thirty feet at first, to provide the overall resolution of the point cloud model. Notice the upper stories of the building façade, which are furthest from the lens. Ample overlap of the images at this point is critical to the overall model, before moving in closer for added detail. Next layer or loop in toward the subject provides the next level of resolution and detail, same overlap, but this time, drawing those points of interest near.[17] This approach closes in any gaps the outer or first layer may not have captured. The students are now finding and seeing detail within the overall context of the building facade. The next layer or loop of images captured occurs with specific focus on entryways, facade materials, and groupings of objects, adding to the overall resolution of the final 3D model.

With focus on the example of the building façade, stepping closer, more focused on image overlap, and now another layer of detail more finite than before, students proceed. Shadow, lack of light, and surface conditions out of site are considered as progress is made. What has been missed? Is the lens able to capture it? The decision to layer in additional loops of images at varying angles is critical at this point of the process to enable the more complex façade objects to exist at a higher resolution in the resulting 3D model. Now, slowing the workflow to close in on the details of each object expands the story being told and requires the student to see what details are hidden. For instance, a stair landing protruding from the building façade, with part walls and rail, will need to be documented with added images, grounding that landing to the walkway in front of it. This is considered as additional layers of images are captured, and focus on the stair landing expands the overall resolution of the 3D model in that location.

Texture, colour, and light continue as an important aspect of finding detail, of the building, and through the lens, in this photogrammetry process. Wrapping layers of images around self-standing objects in front of the building façade subject and filling in the gaps or void areas occur along the way. Further, focusing in on the detail, another level of decisions are made. Is the "micro capture" of the door handles and bolts on the door necessary to the story? How will the students achieve this? Stepping in to yet another layer or loop close to the subject, focus on capturing texture and colour is now more critical than before. Depth of texture within materials such as stone, brick, stucco, and wood is apparent, and continued effort in image overlap is constant. Low light conditions within the details require more images, adding resolution. Door jambs, headers, and thresholds are considered as the images are captured, and the level of detail increases. Wood and stone textures are better revealed in the 3D model, with ample images creating depth of points within the point cloud. What happened to a specific portion of the wood or stone? Is that an important part of the story?

Visualising the point cloud in different forms can be a valuable tool for exploring and understanding the information captured by the lens. By examining the point cloud in the form of a 3D textured mesh, mesh, wireframe, or fully rendered model, the students were able to gain insight into their historic sites at varying scales. This allowed them to see the building's details and unique features and to appreciate its character and history. The different forms of visualisation can provide different perspectives and levels of detail, which can be useful for exploring and analysing the building's design and construction. Through this process, the students were able to deepen their understanding of the building and its history as well as further their knowledge of photogrammetry and 3D modelling.

Challenges in the Field

What worked. What didn't. The field component offers the unique opportunity for experiential learning for the students, involving decisions about camera placement, lighting conditions, and data processing techniques. Performing workflows such as this would originate from virtual learning during COVID-19 times, which is effective only to a certain point. Step-by-step video learning and written content covering terrestrial and aerial photogrammetry and LiDAR scanning workflows were provided by the professor. While only terrestrial photogrammetry was available to the students during their independent field study, the same rules apply to site acquisition and image capture.

What didn't work was the opportunity for exposure to new technology in a given scenario. At the time of COVID, smartphones were only approaching being adequate for use with terrestrial photogrammetry workflows. This is primarily due to technology limitations and if the student had a smartphone with enough resources to accommodate hundreds to thousands of images necessary to capture a chosen subject. At this time, most students were able to utilise a point-and-shoot or DSLR camera to achieve the terrestrial photogrammetry workflows. Procedures would be learned with video learning, trial and error, and reporting findings and 3D point cloud models back to the class and the professor. This proved to be a slow return; however, at the same time, it was a progressive return benefitting learning advancement. Why? Students returning to their independent field study site would need to revisit the number of images, light conditions, and why there is data loss in their 3D point cloud models.

Access to LiDAR 3D laser scanners or UAVs during this time was not an option. This is another level of what did not work to benefit experiential learning. First and foremost, safety, when speaking to the use of UAVs for aerial photogrammetry. Students were not able to perform this workflow as part of their independent field projects. This is a learning opportunity only to be done with the professor present, who, in this case, is a licensed UAV pilot. Student-independent field project sites were chosen by the students themselves, who, during COVID-19 times, were spread across the country. Geography alone contributed to what did not work during this time. Understanding terms and definitions applied to the workflows of terrestrial photogrammetry proved to be a challenge to the students as they were unable to benefit from on-site learning with the class as a whole. It was up to their own interpretation of how they would implement each task assigned. Detailed step-by-step video compositions provided by the professor would become the means of learning and applying the workflows in the field. Reporting back, and repeating this process with feedback, progressed each student forward.

Access to LiDAR 3D laser scanners for any student was not an option during this time solely due to cost and availability. This historically has been a provided resource by the university or professor. Line of site, setup, targeting, and interaction with the technology are integral to experiential learning of the laser scanning process. Step-by-step video learning would enable the students to at least see the workflows through virtual demonstration and then process the supplied LiDAR dataset to process. Gaps or issues with the dataset would not be easily addressed by the students due to not having that opportunity of being in the field with the scanner to see where scan locations had been missed. Site acquisition is only part of the challenge, where what to do with the resulting 3D point cloud from the raw LiDAR data is where the decisions need to be made.

Undertaking an independent terrestrial photogrammetry field study can present a range of challenges and opportunities for students, helping them to develop a more comprehensive understanding of the photogrammetry workflow and its applications. It can also provide them with the opportunity to explore different approaches and techniques for capturing data in the field as well as to develop their problem-solving skills when faced with unexpected challenges. Some of the challenges that students might face when conducting independent fieldwork could include the following:

Time and resource constraints: Conducting a field study can be time-consuming and require significant resources, such as access to specialised equipment and software.

Weather conditions: Weather conditions can have a significant impact on the quality of the data captured through photogrammetry. Adverse weather conditions, such as rain or fog, can make it difficult to capture clear and accurate data.

Site accessibility: Some sites may be difficult to access or present safety hazards, making it challenging for students to capture the data they need. With the support of the class and instructor, site access no longer needs to be achieved alone.

Technical difficulties: Technical difficulties with equipment or software can present challenges for students when conducting independent fieldwork.

By paralleling their in-class fieldwork with independent field study, students can gain a better understanding of what is achievable with terrestrial photogrammetry workflows. They can learn to apply the techniques they have learned in class to real-world scenarios and gain a deeper appreciation of the nuances and complexities of the photogrammetry process. This can help them to develop their skills and knowledge in this area and to become more confident and competent practitioners of terrestrial photogrammetry.

What did work was the learning from the challenge itself. Site choices for student-independent projects would change after their first site acquisition attempt at their first site. What begins as a few dozen images resulting in an incomplete 3D point cloud model becomes hundreds of images in the attempt to capture that first site and complete that same model. This is a pivot point for students and their first time "seeing" the site or subject they are attempting to capture. Light, texture, colour, scale, and access are factors contributing to the success or failure of the capture. The struggle of the capture process alone would cause the students to pivot to a new site to hopefully ensure their success during post-processing of the 3D point cloud model. Ensuring success resulted in more time learning how to implement the processing workflows and point cloud editing. The geographic distance between the students offered a diverse set of projects and site choices; otherwise, it was not seen if we were together physically as a class. The weather alone would be more of a factor depending upon the student's location, which, during this time, was throughout the US. The introduction of independent terrestrial photogrammetry fieldwork during this time would prove to be a task and experience to escalate the students' ability to see the site or subject they are attempting to capture differently. Acknowledging the challenges and nuances of their sites was something they needed to do on their own with provided feedback.

Post-pandemic Teaching

Challenges were faced, lessons learned, and independent terrestrial photogrammetry field study now parallels the in-class fieldwork. This provides unique insight as to what the student might believe they can achieve with the terrestrial photogrammetry workflows.

Now, with the return of in-person instruction supporting fieldwork, those challenges can be addressed with the presence of the professor and support the experiential learning process. Layering on aerial photogrammetry to the student's learning process of terrestrial photogrammetry and LiDAR workflows is best performed in person paired with the class and instructor. Students listen and watch the instructor or classmates as they experience UAV (drone) flight. They then make decisions on factors such as image overlap, altitude, and how to capture the hidden features of the subject or building being surveyed. Terrestrial capture workflows consist of limits in height or how high we can be to gain a good line of site with the lens or laser. The UAV breaks that limit, offering a few of the subjects we would otherwise not be able to acquire. With the addition of the VO (Visual Observer)[18] to support the workflows of UAV flight, students learn to collaborate in the field to successfully acquire the entire site from a heritage standpoint. This process has provided students with new insight into Historic Preservation using point cloud technology, photogrammetry, and 3D laser scanning methods as the vehicle. In an in-person experiential learning process, it is understood that if we simply "hear" information without practical experience, we are more likely to forget it. If we go further and "see" (i.e., study from a book), we will remember it but not grasp it. If we "do" the thing and remember the activity, we will completely understand what we're learning.[19]

Art of the Point Cloud

The true bonus to the entire process was being able to compose and collage through the layered detail of the 3D point cloud. This enabled students to tell the story of their historic site, some of which were inaccessible to anyone at the time. Including a pre-existing image of the interior layered under the front façade, for instance, of their point clouds provided insight as to what resides hidden within and how accurate their point cloud was through the captured datasets. Combining point cloud images with 3D textured mesh, mesh, renders, colour overlay, and real-world or actual images resulted in truly beautiful visuals which would otherwise not be seen or drawn. Taking the benefits of the point cloud this far offered the students a very new and unique way of presentation and drawing composition. This is a step away from the norm. In this section, presentation techniques are introduced to provide the students with an idea of how to represent the densified point clouds. Linear section cuts of the Rough Castle Fort on the Antonine Wall, Scotland,[20] and longitudinal section cuts of the Marble Arch Caves Global Geopark, Northern Ireland, were shown as examples of the point cloud and the beauty that can be achieved with the image showing what could otherwise not be seen from the surface.

Conclusions

The students approached the provided point cloud datasets and their own independent field studies with an investigative eye. By using point clouds, digital terrain models, digital elevation models, digital surface models, and contour line models, they were able to gain a more detailed understanding of their historic sites. The ability to perform accurate measurements and to create 3D textured mesh, animations, and wireframe models allowed students to explore the building at different scales and to see its features from different perspectives. By investigating and critically analysing these forms of data, the students were able to gain a deeper understanding of their historic sites and to make new discoveries about the buildings' design, construction, and history. This demonstrates the value of using advanced technology and techniques in the study of historic buildings. By acknowledging the imperfections, holes, gaps, and missing data within each point cloud dataset, the students were able to identify areas for improvement in their workflows and approach. This shows the importance of critically evaluating the results of the photogrammetry process and recognising any limitations or challenges in the data. To ensure a better result when processing the point cloud, the students may need to consider making changes in various steps of the process. This could include improving the image acquisition process, optimising the data processing techniques, or modifying the methods used to create the 3D models. The specific changes needed will depend on the individual challenges and limitations of each site as well as the student's goals and objectives. However, by actively seeking to improve their workflows and approach, the students can continually refine their skills and techniques and produce better results in the future.

Wildflower Center

The Lady Bird Johnson Wildflower Center[21] at The University of Texas at Austin is the state botanical garden and arboretum of Texas. The centre features more than 900 species of native Texas plants in both garden and natural settings and is home to a breadth of educational programs and events.

Wildflower Center is one of the more complex sites, as it consists of multiple buildings and an expansive landscape. The goal and focus for this site was the interior and exterior of the Wildflower Center central tower. Unlike the Mueller Control Tower's sleek metal and glass façades, the organic stone and brickwork of the tower poses a challenge in assessing how to capture this.

Dual flight path, illustrated in Figure 4.1, provides the best overlap for capturing more surfaces of each building and the tower itself, which is stone.

GCPs

The students learned to make decisions building a thorough ground control point (GCP) layout to ensure the stone tower is well within the triangulation of the UAV flights and 3D laser scans. Each control point resides on a different level, providing a higher level of accuracy for the final densified point cloud. Colour, texture, and proximity to the tower are considered as the GCPs are laid down. Only a few tie points, illustrated in Figure 4.2, are needed at a distance from the tower to provide an additional accuracy check. Discovery of the overall size of the tower is achieved through measurement within the point cloud. GCPs are points on the ground with known coordinates. In an aerial mapping survey, GCPs are points that the surveyor

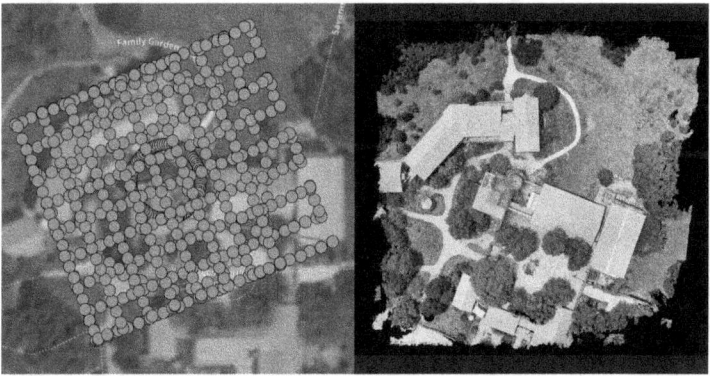

Figure 4.1 Dual flight path for best image overlap. Class: Reality Capture for Architecture, University of Texas at Austin, School of Architecture.

Figure 4.2 Tie Points. Class: Reality Capture for Architecture, University of Texas at Austin, School of Architecture.

can precisely pinpoint: with a handful of known coordinates, it's possible to accurately map large areas.

Animation

Using animation, we visualise the progressive stages of the point cloud from a rough draft with only the automatic tie points calculated, then to the densified point cloud, and finally on to the high-resolution 3D textured mesh, which reveals the detail and colour of the Wildflower Center stone tower.

Vignettes

Using only the densified point cloud, the students learned to build vignette models to achieve views and vantage points of the stone tower, which would otherwise not be possible on the site itself. Using a clipping box as a 3D section cut, we are able to explore those views.

Visualising the 3D Point Cloud

Visualising the 3D Laser Scan Point Cloud, we begin to investigate the material, texture, and spaces of the tower and prove the 3D laser scanner location layout worked. In this view, the small spheres, Figure 4.3, represent the 3D laser scanner locations as a procession climbing the tower's winding staircase. Combining line of site and scanner placement provides the students with the challenge of understanding how to capture a complex space. It is necessary for scan locations to relate to one another and visually connect. Spatial understanding is achieved in detail for students making the scan location decisions. Can we see the prior scan location? Do we have adequate GCPs in place to connect each scan?

A Point Cloud Pedagogy 91

Figure 4.3 Spheres representing 3D laser scanner locations. Class: Reality Capture for Architecture, University of Texas at Austin, School of Architecture.

Visualising Interior Scans

Next, we begin to deconstruct the stone tower by visualising the interior scans as a free-standing model. In this view of the tower, we discover the interior staircase, brick walls, and internal upper chamber without the thick stone skin revealing its own textural personality.

In this image, we can see the centre core of the stone tower captured using a 3D laser scanner. This image is not something that can be seen on-site, as the interior is depicted as a free-standing structure. This is a view of the 3D textured mesh.

Point Cloud Parts

Further deconstructing the internal free-standing model, we can now investigate the large stone wall texture and staircase. The arched stone ceiling is especially interesting as we can now see it on its own. The grey tone point cloud reveals the depth of texture and gradation of the curves in each wall. The upper internal chamber can be investigated and measured as if it were a free-standing structure. This provided the students with great insight into how this stone tower is made and the discovery of a non-symmetrical stair tower. The amorphic stone walls change in thickness, Figure 4.5, throughout which is a condition revealed in the section views of the stair tower. Investigation of the wall texture shows deep reveals and irregular surfacing. This is juxtaposed by the internal brick dome ceiling, which appears symmetrical.

Rendered 3D Mesh

Rendering the free-standing model as 3D vignettes in plan and elevational views, we gain a further understanding of the change in material and depth of the brick and stone textures. The stepped brick in the oculus is very apparent. The brick course change in the main upper chamber shows as a reveal. Understanding the change in texture and building material provides insight as to how the internal chamber is built and where the base of the stair tower tapers to receive the weight from above. The large stone and rough walls at the base show as being wide to provide an adequate foundation. The smaller articulated brick of the internal chamber provides the smooth and curved walls, which gradate to the domed ceiling and finally to the oculus. Understanding the use of each material in those specific conditions provides students with the learning opportunity.

Oculus

In this view, in Figure 4.4, we investigate the centre oculus using a gradated collage of the densified 3D point cloud produced from photogrammetry, 3D laser scans, and still images of the dome itself. This is a result of processing an accurate point cloud and proven with overlaying each method of capture, with the actual image at the end to compare.

Plan Drawings

Deconstructing the point cloud into drawings enabled the students to further investigate the Wildflower Center stone tower. In this view, we pull the tower apart visualising possible levels in plan while revealing the internal chamber and stair. There is now insight on where the internal chamber resides in relation to the outer stone wall. The discovery here is the chamber, stair, and outer wall are not symmetrical within each other.

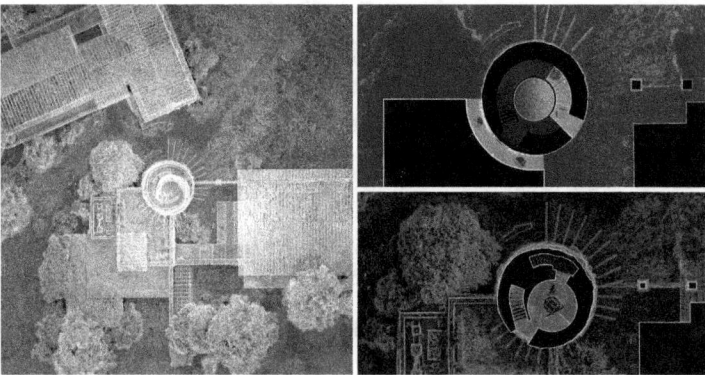

Figure 4.4 Centre oculus using gradated collage. Class: Reality Capture for Architecture, University of Texas at Austin, School of Architecture.

A Point Cloud Pedagogy 93

Figure 4.5 Internal tower of the stair tower chamber. Class: Reality Capture for Architecture, University of Texas at Austin, School of Architecture.

Section

The section drawings tell a revealing story. In Figures 4.5 and 4.6, we overlay the internal chamber 3D laser scans, revealing where the interior resides within the overall tower. Colour mapped to the point cloud allows us to better see the gradation and curves of the chamber and stair tunnel. This set of three drawings are a composition of the densified point cloud generated from both photogrammetry and 3D laser scans along with the building context. There was a story to be told using a combination of 3D laser scanning and photogrammetry. How to set up a procession of scans to ensure the

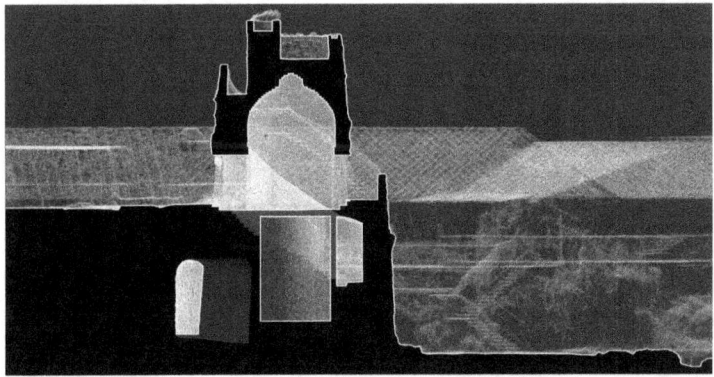

Figure 4.6 Reverse view of internal tower. Class: Reality Capture for Architecture, University of Texas at Austin, School of Architecture.

highest level of detail and texture was seen, and flying the site from above to capture the overall picture provides great insight into what this wildflower centre tower is about.

Plan and Section Drawing Insight

Development of 2D plan and sections drawing provide a next step in the progression of understanding the stone stair tower. To this point, students have investigated the tower in three dimensions. Performing a slice through the 3D model in both a horizontal and vertical format is intended to reveal the potential discoveries within. Students apply colour infill to the void or gaps in the 3D point cloud to discover and measure the widths of the stone walls. Applying elevation labels to the section drawings notes the overall height of the stone stair tower. Multiple slices through the 3D model in plan view provide an abstract view of what the potential levels or floors of the stair tower look like.

Point Cloud Drawing Set

Further refining the densified point cloud into a schematic drawing set, illustrated in Figure 4.7, reveals the detail and accuracy of measurement. The views include axonometric, section, and elevations from the north, south, east, and west, along with three plan drawing levels to complete the schematic set. With this, measurements are made to discover the height of the mid-level and overall height of the stone tower. And taking one more step, we investigate further into the point cloud by using only a section line drawing.

Seaholm Intake Building

Densified point clouds were produced using a combination of 3D laser scans and aerial and terrestrial photogrammetry for the Seaholm Intake Building over the course of a week. This image shows the subterranean chambers, Figure 4.8, which would otherwise not be seen from the exterior.

The Water Intake Structure sits on the shore of Lady Bird Lake, Austin, TX, directly south of the Turbine Generator Building. The structure shares many design and architectural elements with the generator building, with exposed structural concrete walls and large industrial windows opening into a vast interior space. The south face of the building rises two stories above the lake, with ten sluice gates through which cooling water for the plant's steam condensers was taken in. This water was pumped to the generator building through massive underground pipes; after being used as a coolant, the water was discharged into nearby Shoal Creek.

A Point Cloud Pedagogy 95

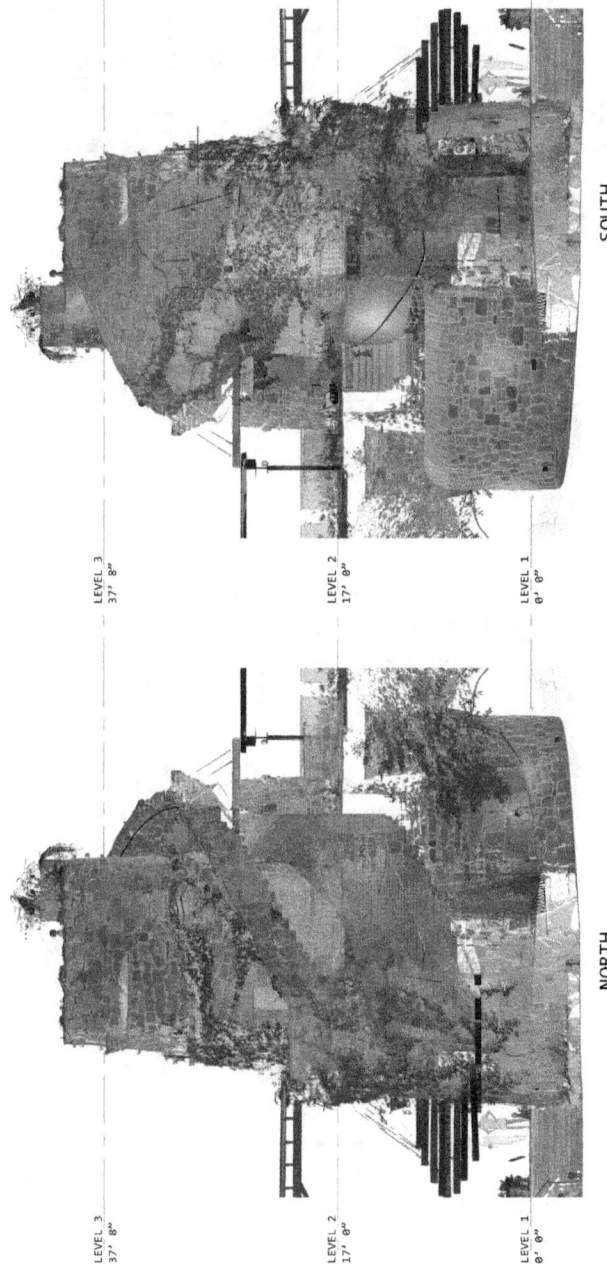

Figure 4.7 Schematic drawing section. Class: Reality Capture for Architecture, University of Texas at Austin, School of Architecture.

96 Robert Stepnoski

Figure 4.8 Subterranean chambers. Class: Reality Capture for Architecture, University of Texas at Austin, School of Architecture.

3D Laser Scan Point Cloud Render

Exploring the 3D laser scan point cloud, we can see the large subterranean lower chambers, Figure 4.7, where the water was fed into the main Seaholm Power Plant Building. The large circles on the lower chamber walls provide clues as to what may have been. The discovery here is the smaller Structure C is not as deep as the other two main chambers. This is a rendered view of the scans, offering detail and accuracy in the concrete texture.

Camera Position

Hundreds of images were taken to provide adequate overlap of the interior photogrammetry. Key decisions are made along the way to ensure the interior concrete texture and surfaces were captured. Several loops and camera angles are seen here as we inspect each tie point for good, accurate coverage. The resulting 3D mesh and textured mesh are accurate. Applying the colour tone study to the model reveals the light sources throughout. Our result is a clean 3D texture mesh model to investigate.

Section Breakaway

This textured mesh section breakaway, as a self-standing model, reveals the subterranean chambers which are otherwise not seen from the outside. At each section cut, there is the opportunity to investigate each floor, façade, fenestration, and concrete texture. The opening in the floor is clear in this view, as well as the slots in the perimeter floor, which is currently covered with plywood. Historically, each slot held a piece of machinery supporting the function of the building.

Waterfront Façade

The waterfront façade could only be captured by using a UAV. In this case, the UAV was flown manually along the front of the façade to capture as much detail as possible. A high level of image overlap was used to ensure the façade's concrete reveals would exist in the point cloud model.

Interior Perspective

In this view, the interior was captured using all three methods of acquisition. The challenges here are to find a way to document the hidden concrete ledges which are out of reach from both the camera and 3D laser scanner. Precise flight of the UAV was the choice to fill the voids of the interior surfaces, knowing there will be some aspects missed. Inspection of the image overlap provide good insight into ensuring an accurate point cloud of the space.

Building C

Building C of the Seaholm Intake Building provides its own set of digital documentation challenges where machinery obstructions exist throughout. Precise flight of the UAV was required to capture the upper concrete surfaces accurately. Several layers of loops around the space and multiple camera angles were used to capture the hidden surfaces throughout. This resulted in a great level of image tie point overlap, Figure 4.9, providing an accurate point cloud and clean 3D textured mesh. Building C was the smallest structure of the two to be built as part of the Seaholm Intake Building. It provided the exit for the water used to cool the main Seaholm Power Plant building.

Figure 4.9 Building C, loops of images. Class: Reality Capture for Architecture, University of Texas at Austin, School of Architecture.

Notes

1. Robert Stepnoski. "Seaholm Investigation Video: Seaholm Intake Building | Photogrammetry, LiDAR, UAV Flight Acquisition, Point Cloud". https://youtu.be/n0kprbhZXd8
2. Robert Stepnoski. "Reality Capture for Architecture 2019 | Stepnoski". 2019. https://youtu.be/dZt_00RI0MY
3. University of Texas at Austin, School of Architecture. "Realty Capture for Architecture". 2019. https://soa.utexas.edu/reality-capture-architecture
4. UNESCO. World Heritage Foundation. Concept of Digital Heritage. UNESCO 2019. "Is there an emerging digital heritage?" Accessed 2019. https://en.unesco.org/themes/information-preservation/digital-heritage/concept-digital-heritage
5. Jon Baginski. "Practical Photogrammetry — Digitizing Real-world places". Accessed 2019. https://medium.com/@jonbaginski/practical-photogrammetry-digitising-real-world-places-59991770cab0
6. UNESCO. World Heritage Foundation. Concept of Digital Heritage. UNESCO 2019. "Is there an emerging digital heritage?" Accessed 2019. https://en.unesco.org/themes/information-preservation/digital-heritage/concept-digital-heritage
7. UNESCO World Heritage Convention. "Sydney Opera House". Accessed 2019/2020. https://whc.unesco.org/en/list/166/
8. American Battles Monuments Commission. "Meuse-Argonne American Cemetery". Accessed October 29, 2020. https://www.abmc.gov/Meuse-Argonne
9. UNESCO. World Heritage Foundation. Outstanding Universal Value, Synthesis. "Monastery of Geghard and the Upper Azat Valley". Accessed Summer 2019/2020. https://whc.unesco.org/en/list/960
10. ScienceNews Nonprofit Organization. "Lidar Reveals the Oldest and Biggest Maya Structure yet Found". Accessed June 2020. https://www.sciencenews.org/article/lidar-reveals-oldest-biggest-ancient-maya-structure-found-mexico
11. Towers. "After 15 Years of Mueller, Its Iconic Control Tower Has Never Looked Better". Accessed 2019/2020. https://austin.towers.net/after-15-years-of-mueller-its-iconic-control-tower-has-never-looked-better/
12. The Portal To Texas History. "Littlefield Carriage House". Accessed 2019. https://texashistory.unt.edu/ark:/67531/metapth667195/
13. Austin Park and Recreation. "Seaholm Intake Facility". Accessed 2019. https://www.austintexas.gov/page/seaholm-intake-facility
14. Trevor English. Interesting Engineering. "What Is LiDAR Technology and What Are Its Main Applications?" Accessed 2020. https://interestingengineering.com/science/what-is-lidar-technology-and-what-are-its-main-applications
15. Sketchfab. "Lighting in Photogrammetry". Accessed 2019. https://sketchfab.com/blogs/community/lighting-in-photogrammetry/
16. Robert Stepnoski. "Terrestrial Photogrammetry Facade | Reality Capture for Architecture". Accessed 2019. https://www.youtube.com/watch?v=fHmMSVMLD94
17. Cultural Heritage Imaging. "Photogrammetry Image Collection Basics". Accessed 2019. https://vimeo.com/243723243
18. Federal Aviation Administration. "Small Unmanned Aircraft Systems (UAS) Regulations (Part 107)". Updated Tuesday, October 6, 2020. https://www.faa.gov/newsroom/small-unmanned-aircraft-systems-uas-regulations-part-107
19. Grammarhow. "I Hear And I Forget. I See And I Remember. I Do And I Understand." Meaning & Origin". Accessed 2019. https://grammarhow.com/i-hear-and-i-forget-i-see-and-i-remember-i-do-and-i-understand-meaning-origin/
20. Paul Chapman, David Mitchell, Chris McGregor, Lynne Wilson and Alastair Rawlinson. "Art of the Point Cloud" (Glasgow: Wild Harbour, 2018), 170, 171.
21. Wikipedia. "Lady Bird Johnson Wildflower Center". Description. Mission. History. Accessed 2019. https://www.ladybirdjohnson.org

Bibliography

American Battles Monuments Commission. 2020. "Meuse-Argonne American Cemetery". Accessed October 29, 2020. https://www.abmc.gov/Meuse-Argonne

Chapman, Paul, David Mitchell, Chris McGregor, Lynne Wilson and Alastair Rawlinson. "Art of the Point Cloud". Glasgow: Wild Harbour, 2018.

Cultural Heritage Imaging. 2017. Non-Profit Organization. Date: Unknown. "Photogrammetry". Accessed June 1, 2019. https://vimeo.com/243723243

Curbed Austin. February 2018. "Mueller tower could become landmark open to public". Classic midcentury design by Fehr & Granger. Accessed June 15, 2020. https://austin.curbed.com/2018/2/27/17060042/austin-midcentury-modern-landmark-mueller-fehr-granger

Curbed Austin. June 2017. "Intake buildings and surrounding parkland discussed". Accessed June 2019/2020. https://austin.curbed.com/2017/6/26/15876940/austin-seaholm-redevelopment-intake-photos

CyArk Nonprofit Organization. "Monastery of Geghard". In-depth, Architectural Influence. Accessed, June 2019/2020. https://www.cyark.org/projects/monastery-of-geghard/in-depth

GIM International. GIS Geography. 2010. Last Updated: October 29, 2020. "OBIA – Object-Based Image Analysis (GEOBIA). Think Objects, Not Pixels". Accessed, May 5, 2021. https://www.gim-international.com/content/article/object-based-image-analysis

Medium. Stories, thinking, and expertise from writers on any topic. Jon Baginski. "Practical Photogrammetry—Digitizing Real-world places". 2017 Online Journal. Accessed, June 15, 2019. https://medium.com/@jonbaginski/practical-photogrammetry-digitising-real-world-places-59991770cab0

National Geographic. "Massive 3,000-year-old ceremonial complex discovered in 'plain sight'. 2020. Accessed, June 2020. https://www.nationalgeographic.com/history/article/massive-ancient-maya-ceremonial-complex-discovered-hiding-plain-sight

National Park Service. US Department of the Interior. HABS/HAER/HALS. 3D Laser Scan model and animation walkthrough. 2016 "Meuse-Argonne American Cemetery & Memorial". Accessed Summer 2019/2020. https://www.youtube.com/watch?v=hoZccKLWLpA

Pix4D. Photogrammetry Software Technology. 2019. "What is ground control point in photogrammetry?" Accessed October 20, 2023. https://www.pix4d.com/blog/why-ground-control-points-important/

Pix4D. Photogrammetry Software Technology. October 30, 2019. "GIS: Grave Information Systems". Accessed June 1, 2020. https://www.pix4d.com/blog/gis-grave-information-systems/

ScienceNews Nonprofit Organization. 2020. "Lidar reveals the oldest and biggest Maya structure yet found". Accessed, June 1, 2020. https://www.sciencenews.org/article/lidar-reveals-oldest-biggest-ancient-maya-structure-found-mexico

Statesman. September 2018. "Austin's 1960s Mueller airport control tower getting retro restoration". Accessed June 1, 2020. https://www.statesman.com/story/business/2012/09/01/austins-1960s-mueller-airport-control-tower-getting-retro-restoration/9945211007/

Studio Gang. 2018. "Seaholm Waterfront Concept Study". Accessed June 10, 2019. https://studiogang.com/project/seaholm-waterfront-concept-study

Sydney Opera House to Australia. "Sydney Opera House, World Heritage". Accessed May 2019/2020. https://www.sydneyoperahouse.com/our-story/conserving-and-celebrating-our-heritage

The Austin Chronicle. June 2018. "New Life for Seaholm Power Plant? Seaholm Intake Building". Accessed January 2019/2020. https://www.austinchronicle.com/daily/news/2018-06-04/new-life-for-seaholm-power-plant/

The English Shed. "The Scottish Ten". Sydney Opera House project documentation source. Accessed June 2019/2020. https://www.engineshed.scot/about-us/the-scottish-ten/?id=32394

The Portal to Texas History. University of North Texas Libraries. December 1950. "Seaholm Power Plant Intake Facility". Accessed 2019. https://texashistory.unt.edu/ark:/67531/metapth124841/

Towards Data Science. April 2020. "The Future of 3D Point Clouds: A New Perspective". Accessed June 2019. https://medium.com/towards-data-science/the-future-of-3d-point-clouds-a-new-perspective-125b35b558b9

Towards Data Science Inc. May 2019. "How to represent 3D data". Accessed June 2019. https://towardsdatascience.com/how-to-represent-3d-data-66a0f6376afb

UNESCO. World Heritage Foundation. "Cuilcagh Lakelands UNESCO Global Geopark (Ireland & United Kingdom of Great Britain and Northern Ireland)". Accessed June 1, 2019. https://en.unesco.org/global-geoparks/marble-arch-caves

UNESCO. World Heritage Foundation. Concept of Digital Heritage. UNESCO 2019. "Is there an emerging digital heritage?" Accessed June 20, 2019. https://en.unesco.org/themes/information-preservation/digital-heritage/concept-digital-heritage

UNESCO. World Heritage Foundation. Discussion Paper on Digital Preservation. March 2020. *"What is preservation of digital heritage"*. pp. 5–7.

UNESCO. World Heritage Foundation. 2000. Outstanding Universal Value, Synthesis. "Monastery of Geghard and the Upper Azat Valley". Accessed June 20, 2019. https://whc.unesco.org/en/list/960

UNESCO World Heritage Status. CyArk Nonprofit Organization. 2013. "Sydney Opera House". Accessed 2019/2020. https://www.cyark.org/projects/sydney-opera-house/overview

University of Texas at Austin. UT Maps. "Littlefield Carriage House". Accessed July 1, 2020. https://utdirect.utexas.edu/apps/campus/buildings/nlogon/maps/UTM/LCH/

Wikipedia. "Lady Bird Johnson Wildflower Center". Description. Mission. History. Accessed June 1, 2019. https://www.ladybirdjohnson.org

5 Observing/Performing the (Pandemic) Every Day

Photographic Writing as a Curating Tool in Online Architectural Education

Bilge Beril Kapusuz Balci

Introduction

The intertwined relationship between photography and architecture has a long history not only in terms of communication, documentation, and critical reinterpretation of the built environment but also in educational terms. Regarding the significance of photography in teaching the history of architecture, the experience of the artefacts through their images disseminated through lecture slides, books, and journals has become a convention, replacing the direct experience. However, using photography as a pedagogical tool and encouraging students to "make" photographs as an alternative to their passive looking or reading of them assign the students the status of "active observers" and provide a performative and participatory mode of learning. Through their observations and photographic notetakings on their environment that involves their bodily presence with a creative and interpretative approach, a holistic view of architecture and the city is enabled: The transformation and appropriation of the buildings, urban and natural landscape with everyday life practices become visible through photographic research, and overstepping the conventional use of photography that portrays the formal qualities of architecture. Therefore, the traditional learning space expands from the design studio/class to the city and everyday life, where the agencies of the architects and the built environment are redistributed using space and the passage of time.

The long-standing and complex connection between photography and architectural education has been given new consideration in the era of digital photography and the increased dissemination of architectural photographs on social media. With the emergence of new lines of inquiry into photography's ongoing influence on architectural theory, practice, and education, this relationship grew more complex throughout the peculiar and unique context of the pandemic. Considering the preceding, this chapter explores the pedagogical strategies and learning outcomes of the author's "Image Construction and Architectural Photography" course at Gazi University's Faculty of Architecture, taught online during the COVID-19 lockdown.

DOI: 10.4324/9781003435396-6

The chapter will present how the course expands the research fields in architectural education, reaching out to fields of architecture, urban studies, and visual culture through an ethnographic lens using photography. It will also show how it decentralises the limited online learning space throughout the pandemic while presenting a critical overview of the accomplishments and inconsistencies of the method and its post-COVID reflections.

The course assigns architectural photography an agency in understanding the built environment as a complex form of social and spatial practices, unlike the conventional use of the medium as a sole representation of static artefacts. Drawing on Bruno Latour and Albena Yaneva's perspective on the day-to-day ethnography of buildings in terms of writing and visualising space, the course brought forward the observation of "the every day" in the photographic narration of the architectural space. It gave students a critical and performative tool for writing architecture as a visual language.

The students were expected to observe the pandemic every day, recapturing an urban scene/fragment in their neighbourhood for 30 days, yet performing an alternative daily routine. Photography became a mediating tool between observation and critical performance, while photographic writing provided the student with an alternative tool for researching the multiple forms of space in use. This chapter will suggest that photographic reports had a two-fold agency as a "curating" tool in online architectural education. It operates as a method to curate the (pandemic) everyday life in unfamiliar uses of familiar spaces for students and to cure and heal their palsied everyday life. It is a performative and reformative learning process in which the students are both the curator and the fixed. Finally, this chapter will argue that this process extends beyond the pandemic condition and online teaching; it can construct a pedagogical framework focusing on the relationship between photography and everyday life while drawing attention to the stimulating and curative effect of the everyday. The reiterative photographic performances alternate their daily routines and how they experience their immediate environment; the students practice carrying a critical "lens" directed to the everyday matters of the built environment to better read, analyse, and interpret its multiple dimensions and agencies involved. Thus, beyond how the method operated in the lockdown period and online education, it can also be approached in a broader context regarding its potential in architectural education to take full advantage of photography's agency in visual research and storytelling.

Paralysis: Pandemic Every Day and Immobility of Online Architectural Education

In her article "Choreographies for the Laboratorized City", published in *Architectural Theory Review* during the COVID-19 pandemic, Yaneva discusses the transformative effect of the virus on our everyday routines. Laboratorising the urban space and architecture typologies, the virus created a new choreography in daily life due to various distancing measures.¹ She questions how this "enigmatic nonhuman actor changes practical settings and epistemic formats of architectural practice" and how it "modifies the meaning of the social for social studies of design". Since the same questions might also apply to educational ecologies of design, one of the remarks she makes becomes very significant for the subject matter of this chapter: Yaneva argues that the social dimension of architecture and urban design is now of primary importance that requires a reconsideration.[2]

In the spring of 2021, one year after the outbreak of the COVID-19 pandemic, many universities were still teaching online, and Gazi University Faculty of Architecture in Ankara (Turkey) was one of those offering the courses via digital video-oriented platforms. Originally from different cities in Turkey, the students were already back in their hometowns due to the uncertain situation about the normalisation process, each participating in the virtual classes from their workspaces that were inevitably embedded in their domestic environment. It is possible to mention paralysis in their everyday life with an online workload. Their academic performance and interaction were limited to verbal and visual expressions, eliminating bodily form.

The elective course conducted by the author in the same faculty, entitled Image Construction and Architectural Photography, was also one of the online courses offered in the 2020–2021 Spring semester. The course is the subject of this chapter in terms of its concerns about immobile online architectural education and its very intentions to alter the ongoing computer-oriented teaching/learning environment while including those diverse spatial and social contexts in which the students were engaged. The pre-pandemic version of the course was occupied with the representation of architecture and photographic narration of space – through students' on-site work in specific buildings, namely museums and art galleries in Ankara – mostly in its formal and material forms. However, through the pandemic, the quarantine measures disrupted the existing method of the course. Since buildings, regarded as "pedagogical" and defined as visual research fields within the course's scope, were inaccessible, teaching architectural photography became problematic. The students could only access their immediate environment by walking for a limited time during the weekdays. However, in parallel with Yaneva's remark, the course reintroduced the students' limited but accessible built environment as an expanded field of learning and rethinking architecture: The aim was to make students decipher the evident social dimensions of urban settings "as architectural knowledge is embodied in people and things, made through mundane and locally varying modes of social and cultural interaction".[3]

In this regard, the following questions were posed in structuring the course in a new context: How can it expand the field and practices of palsied everyday life with the space of pandemic teaching/learning? Can we create an alternative daily routine instrumentalising photography as a habitual act of engaging with the immediate environment? Is it possible to attribute an agency to the course and to "photography as a pedagogical tool" to improve students' well-being while offering an instrument to take a fresh and critical look at the neighbourhood they live in or are stuck in? How could these spatial explorations be displayed through shared tools and languages?

Around these questions, the structure of the course was modified to the existing pandemic conditions. Under normal conditions, the course had a tripartite structure: (1) theoretical background with a series of lectures accompanied by photographic submissions students are required to do weekly, (2) announcement of the final photographic project focusing on specific buildings or places under a common theme, and (3) curating a group exhibition that accommodated all the photographic works of the students. A reappropriated version of the course inverted the structure and methods, assigning students their unique immediate environments from the beginning of the course as they were expected to explore through photographic means daily, articulating urban exploration into their pandemic everyday life through observation and performance. The main goal of the course was to involve students deeply in architectural photography, enabling them to perceive their immediate urban environments through a creative lens and respond to the challenges posed by the pandemic.

Pedagogies of an Alternative Daily Routine: Observing/ Performing the Pandemic Everyday through Photography

In her book *Places of Learning: Media, architecture, pedagogy,* Elizabeth Ellsworth argues that it is possible to speak of pedagogy indirectly through various forms of design and experience and considers both places and events, both built environment and performances "as being pedagogical".[4] Ellsworth notes as follows:

> The places of learning that I have considered here address us in ways that put to powerful use the understanding that learning involves cognition — but never direct, unmediated cognition. Learning never occurs without bodies, emotions, place, time, sound, image, self-experience, and history. It always detours through memory, forgetting, desire, fear, pleasure, surprise, and rewriting. And, because learning always takes place in relation, its detours take us up to and sometimes across the boundaries of habit, recognition, and the socially constructed identities within ourselves. Learning takes us up to and across the boundaries between ourselves and others and through the place of culture and the time of history.[5]

In another recent body of work on architectural pedagogy, *Emerging Practices in Architectural Pedagogy: Accommodating an Uncertain Future,* Laura

Sanderson and Sally Stone draw attention to the move from a "fact-based acquisition process" to a "participatory method of learning" and highlight the responsibility of students of architecture in critically rethinking the built environment through examination and analysis of the existing situation to come up with an alternative perspective; they denote as follows: "students must be enquiring, activist and vigilant".[6] Another critical remark is on the significance of developing an "awareness of socio-cultural and environmental issues",[7] which is reframed in this chapter and within the scope of the course in a micro-scale of daily life and the immediate environment.

As proposed in the title of this chapter, informed by ethnographic and artistic methods, photographic writing is introduced as a pedagogical tool through observation and performance of the pandemic everyday life. As conceptualised and instrumental, photographic writing draws upon Eduardo Cadava's conception of photography that conceives images into a means of profound communication and intellectual discourse, providing viewers with avenues for contemplation, analysis, and emotional connection. Photography, coupled with the act of writing, is here suggested to have a two-folded operation as observation and performance. Photographic writing is valued as a learning tool for students to visually write about architecture, the city, and urban life in their immediate environment in a habitual pattern. In this sense, the concepts of time, space, and repetition in architecture and socio-material notions of urban reality are further discussed through the textual, photographic, and curatorial expression of the students who attended the course.[8]

Observation: Immediate Environment as an Expanded Field/ Space of Pandemic Everyday/Learning

Yaneva draws attention to the shift that occurred in contemporary urban theory, which focuses on the agency of the material aspects of the urban setting, such as the life of the built environment and the lives of the inhabitants.[9] Architecture as a static entity or a mere artefact is brought into question in an expanded field of disciplines from cultural geography to archaeology and sociology and redefined as a dynamic and ongoing process that necessitates a more profound understanding through "tracing the paths and flows of nonhumans that circulate within cities". Informed by the works of Bruno Latour and his Actor-Network-Theory, Yaneva defines *architecture* as an "ecology of practice":

> It is a new way to handle all the objects of human and non-human collective life. To view architecture as an "ecology of practice" means redefining the complicated associations between its beings: habits, skills, buildings, sites, city regulations, designers' equipment, clients, institutions, models, images, urban visions, and landscapes. "Ecology" dissolves boundaries and redistributes agency.[10]

Accordingly, in her chapter Politics of Architectural Imaging, Four Ways of Assembling a City, Yaneva attributes an agency to the images of architecture in "tracing the urban" and assembling the city with various notions of urban life. Rather than mere symbolic representations of the buildings, Yaneva calls for images of architecture that "represent themselves, through their atmospheric, social, cultural and informative layers that address an ecology of social and material relationships between the buildings and the urban reality".[11] As mentioned, Yaneva appropriates the actor–network theory (ANT) methodology by documenting the "interesting stories" that the building unfolds through her fieldwork as a self-observer, tracing and describing the interactions and mediations between other people's daily routines, her own, and the design objects/spaces. This approach allows her to explore the network of relations, wherein each assemblage constructs its narrative locally, leading to the exposure of diverse narrations rather than a singular, univocal theory. By immersing herself in the actors' worlds and capturing their implicit theories in their native words, the ANT methodology facilitates the generation of multiple implicit theories, better suited to elucidate the intricacies of the actors' world-building activities. She conducts a daily ethnography of the building as an ethnographer and storyteller on the network that supports the building through writing, whether in literary or visual forms.[12] As an ethnographer, she engages in a day-to-day ethnography of the building and as a storyteller on the network that makes the building work using the act of writing, be it in visual or literary forms. By linking to the characteristics of the Euclidian space of architectural representation, Latour and Yaneva (2008) challenge the static perspective of artefacts in their essay "Give me a gun, and I will make all buildings move": An ANT's view of architecture. Recalling the "gun" mentioned by the authors in the title of their remarkable article refers to the chronophotographic technique developed by the French scientist Etienne Jules Marey, also known as the "photo-graphic-gun" by Latour and Yaneva. Marey used this technique to record multiple stages of a continuous flow of movement in a single format. The writers discuss Marey's chronophotography when discussing the necessity for a tool that can show a building as "a moving project".[13]

Drawing upon Latour and Yaneva's emphasis on the dynamic nature of the ecology of the built environment and the problem of its representation, observation through time and repetition is introduced to the students as an act of direct experience of their immediate environment, which is defined as the expanded field of their pandemic everyday life and learning environment. This observation required a "thick time", referring to Jeremy Till's terms, for the transient nature of everyday life practices, assigning it a habitual character. Till's idea of "thick time" concerning photography might involve capturing images that go beyond the superficial appearance of a place. Instead, the photographs could aim to depict the layers of history, culture, and social dynamics that have shaped the environment being photographed. Using photography as a tool to explore the complexity of a site over time, "thick time" could involve creating visual narratives with a deeper understanding of the historical and cultural contexts within which architectural spaces exist.

Furthermore, "thick time" refers to the notion that a building's value and meaning are not static but constantly changing and open to interpretation. A building may be experienced quite differently by various people at various times and circumstances. Through observation in thick time, the expanded space of the learning environment mediates an expanded present that allows diverse temporal conditions to coexist and unfold. In parallels with Latour and Yaneva's critical approach to the built environment, Till's expanded definition of architecture provides a coherent framework as well; the author argues as follows:

> Architecture needs to be a setting that allows these diverse temporal conditions to coexist. Not just the event but the potential for the event being overlaid on a regular ritual. Not just a building that responds to cyclic rhythms (of life, of the seasons, of the world), but one that allows these to unfold against the linear aspects (of decay, of change). Time places architecture in a dynamic continuity in its connectedness, aware of the past projecting to the future. The here-and-now is seen not as an instant to be satisfied but as part of an "expanded present" or of what may be designated "Thick Time."[14]

Performance: Photographic Writing as a Pedagogical Tool

Photography, of two Greek words, *photos*, which is light, and *graphe*, which is writing, has been conceptualised by the literature professor Eduardo Cadava through "light writing". As Cadava refers to and adapts, Talbot defines the medium of photography as "words of light".[15] Thinking about photography as a visual performance of writing, a single photograph corresponds to a word. In contrast, a series of photographs correspond to a sentence or a statement, yet to sentences or narration. Informed by this theoretical framework, *architectural photography* is defined in the course as a performance of photographic writing on architecture by constructing narrations. In this regard, photographic writing as a visual research method offers students a better understanding of their immediate environment, addressing its pedagogical potential in architectural education.

As a "practical ecology", photography includes multiplicities such as the photographer subject, the temporal-spatial context of the photographed, and the complex production processes, including the mechanical camera, the light, and the frame. Shifting the focus of photography from the "photograph as an object" to the "making of photography as a process" highlights the performative character of photography.[16] Questioning the relationship between photography and performance, Ian Wiblin also addresses the photographer's presence and role "through the intentionality and implied physicality"; he considers photography as an action becoming a performance in terms of the temporal co-acting of mind, eye, and the human body.[17] Accordingly, Wiblin states as follows:

> The camera's operation creates a distance between myself and my subject, but it also generates an intensity of experience. Through such experience, I am automatically implicated in the photographs I take and make.[18]

Discussing the role of photography in architectural education through their teaching practices, Selay Yurtkuran Tok et al. point out the significance of visual thinking in architecture and the potential of photography as a mode of visual thinking for critical insight and interpretation of the built environment in its social layers, instead of the conventional use of the medium as a form of documentation and illustration of the material aspects.[19] Abeer Elshater, drawing upon her own experience in teaching photography and urban design, discusses the power of photography as a teaching method and technique occupied with the city and considers the photographic method as a "communication routine" through establishing dialogues with the everyday events that form urban life.[20] In another notable scholarship on the pedagogical agencies of photography, Pedro Leão Neto et al. discuss their pedagogical experience to foster critical awareness about architecture and public space as an evolving and upgraded methodology for teaching technical and artistic aspects of photography and for discussing photography projects through creating and communicating visual narratives on architecture and urban culture. According to the authors, using photography as a pedagogical tool encouraged students' participation outside the conventional time and space of the classes, providing them with a means to create "visual narratives for appraisal, analysis and perception of certain public spaces and architecture".[21]

In this sense, complementary to the act of passive observation in ethnographic terms, photography as a performance enhances students' critical and active engagement with their environment if conducted as a part of their daily routine while creating visual narratives or photographic writings as defined in this chapter and provides them tools to decipher the "thickness" of time and space. The bodily and social presence of the photographer subject and intellectual stance become a part of the visual construction of the photograph: The students physically and intellectually are a part of the performative and critical act as a reflection of a participatory mode of learning, in which they are in a constant dialogue with their environment (Figure 5.1).

Figure 5.1 Phase 1: Cure for the self: "The Square: The Heart" by Zeynep Coşkuner.

Curating: "Cure for the Self/City"

Today, *curating* is defined in a transdisciplinary field as a professional practice and research method, "a tool that could be employed by architects [...] by all those figures responsible for shaping the built environment".[22] Curating has become a "process of display and interpretation" for which the contemporary city could be approached "as a collection to be curated".[23] Referring to the connotations of care and responsibility, curating becomes very relevant as a tool for the multi-layered and hybrid urban reality in pedagogical terms, especially in peculiar times of pandemic when both the students and their surrounding environment needed healing. The significance of the curating led to the title of the students' final exhibition as one outcome of the course, "Cure for the Self/City". The final project of the course assigned aimed to "heal the city" by documenting the pandemic's impact on their immediate environment. It served as both a therapeutic process for the students and a visual representation of their experiences. The work by the students will be covered in the following.

Following the 30 days observation and photographic writing on the "site", the students chose their neighbourhoods; the outcome was 28 different photographic series from 28 unique urban settings, displayed as two environments:

The first environments were in-situ works, in which the students displayed their printed photographic series where they had been conducting their visual research. Setting up their petit exhibition in the public space, informed by their spatial research on the site that they had been observing and recording daily, constituted the curatorial work they were expected to produce. On the one hand, this part of their final project was an attempt to "cure the city" they lived in throughout the pandemic on a limited part of their immediate environment they were critically engaged with. On the other hand, the photographic series exhibited became the visual documents of their healing process that tried to cure their very own selves and their paralysed everyday life through the intrusion of photography into their daily routine, making their physical performance a part of the process.

The second environment was the digital space of Instagram, where their works were archived in the feed of the Instagram profile of the course M3802 and displayed as a unity; it is the final exhibition entitled "Cure for the Self/ City".[24] Each curatorial work is accessible through two phases in two different posts: The first phase, "curing the self", presents a selection of their daily photographs one after another, while the second phase, "curing the city", presents their in-situ work in the form of an installation photograph from the former environment as their *petit*-exhibition, accompanied with the titles and short texts of the work.

The installation photograph as the outcome of the second phase not only documented the ephemeral presence of their exhibition but also gave clues about the multiple ways of perceiving the place they were habitually connected to. The arrangement of the installation photos visually conveyed the students' interpretation of the space's physical and social aspects. These reflective images bridge various exploration sites and the digital exhibition, providing additional insights to online viewers. Almost like *mies-en-abyme* and a meditative act, in the installation photograph, the image of the place is doubled multiple times through the series of photographs, where the photograph's content is the photograph itself. This reflexive photograph of the exhibition environment mediates between the various sites of exploration and the digital space, which offers further investigation for the online visitors of the final exhibition (Figure 5.2).

To mention a few works, it is possible to define urban spaces subject to day-to-day photographic writing under "gathering spaces", such as squares or parks, "transitional spaces", such as pedestrian crossings or sidewalks, and in-between spaces, such as sideway parking and entranceways, between blocks. In one of the two works focusing on gathering spaces, the student observes a park parallel to the sidewalk that he uses daily as an alternative to the sidewalk (Figure 5.3). Through framing this pond every day, his regular visit to the site gives him a critical insight into the ontology of this pond

Observing/Performing the (Pandemic) Every Day 111

Figure 5.2 Exhibition poster and the digital exhibition environment.

he has not thought about before, making him question its functions beyond intention and how it becomes an incidental agent of unexpected uses and interactions.[25] Adopting an object-oriented approach, the photographic series tells us the story of an urban "thing" that illustrates confusion regarding aesthetics, functionality, and use.

Figure 5.3 Phase 2: Cure for the City: "Confusion" by Hüseyin Avni Halıcı.

Figure 5.4 Phase 2: Cure for the City: "The Square: The Heart" by Zeynep Coşkuner.

Another work, also focusing on a gathering space, aims to adopt an environmental approach to understanding the multiple layers of an urban setting, framing a public square. The student's photographic series tells the stories of human and non-human entities in co-living, sharing the same square; photographic writings at different times of the day make notes on the presence of the tables, chairs, pigeons, the mosque, other buildings, the people, and the atmosphere (Figure 5.4). As stated in the text by the student, different possible stories that she would witness, even the different atmospheric conditions that the square would reflect, transformed this reiterative performance into an aspirational action with environmental awareness.[26]

Other examples of works include a decision to stop and observe around at a transitional space the others pass by. Resisting the intentionality of the spaces that indicate a constant flux, the student's counter-intuition to stop and take photographic notes of those spaces triggers a critical look supported by physical performance. The first and second phases of curating in the space of movement and flow create a conflict when the others stop by to view the photographs displayed. With an analytical approach, one of the works frames the roundabout and the pedestrian cross, also including a convex mirror in the frame that shows another off-frame scene. His observation of this space at different times of the day seeks to understand the daily cycle of the space concerning the cars, bicycles, and pedestrians inhabiting the roads and the buildings around[27] (Figure 5.5). The other work transforms two phases into activism to draw attention to the ongoing urban transformation in her hometown. Her decision to observe the dynamic, everchanging, and live city from a reflection, facing her camera towards the glass surface of an uninhabited shop on the street level, attributes a two-fold agency to the reflective surface she faces daily. The glass becomes a mediator that creates a critical distance between the "matter of concern" and her while including her bodily presence in the photographs she makes daily with the built

Figure 5.5 Phase 2: Cure for the City: "Crossroads" by Eren Burak Çöplü.

environment surrounding her. The materiality of the surface, as declared in the manifesto of the work as the student calls it, when reflecting light, renders her image visible, making her a part of the ongoing urban life in the frame or under different light conditions and erases all photos, giving a view of the empty room instead. Installing her photographic series on this surface materialises this dialogue between the everchanging observer and the observed[28] (Figure 5.6).

One last work to mention focuses on an in-between space, the void between two apartment blocks in the neighbourhood. Through the student's observations, she aims to frame the void defined by the surrounding facades of the blocks and the balconies standing over the void to understand the various ways this void mediates between three facades that accommodate windows and semi-private balconies of multiple households and to question existent and potential spatial agencies of this repeating constituent of the urban reality. Through the photographic writing, she notes how disconnected the inhabitants

Figure 5.6 Phase 2: Cure for the city: "Mirror mirror on the wall who is the fastest city of them all?" by Dilannur Özdemir.

Figure 5.7 Phase 2: Cure for the City: "Gap" by Yaşanur Çil.

are; although facing the same space, balconies, too, are idle. The printed photographic series telling the quotidian stories of the space are displayed on one of the side walls to direct the temporary users or pass inhabitants to stop and take a closer look at the photographs since she intentionally prints them in a 35-mm film roll format that promises the show how the space is transformed daily[29] (Figure 5.7).

Concluding Remarks

The elective course Image Construction and Architectural Photography, with its pedagogical agency and the outcomes in strange times such as the pandemic, is discussed as the subject matter of this chapter. Referring to the questions and problems posed by the course, students were offered an expanded pandemic everyday life and a flexible alternative to the limited physical space of pandemic online education. Defining architectural photography as a "making" process, the students as the photographers were involved through their educated/critical eye and their performing bodies. They reassembled the urban setting within the camera frame, approaching photography as a compositional writing tool through observation and performance. Accordingly, photographic writing operated as a learning tool to write about architecture and the city visually and urban life in their immediate environment in a habitual and healing pattern.

Their final project made a small-scale effort to "cure the city" of the immediate environment they were vitally engaged with during the pandemic. At the same time, the photographic series displayed on the digital space of social media served as the visual representation of their therapeutic process, which attempted to "cure very own selves and their paralysed everyday life" by bringing photography into their daily lives and integrating their first-hand knowledge and physical performance into the process itself. The installation photo captured the exhibition's momentary existence and provided information on numerous viewpoints on the location that preoccupied the students regularly.

The arrangement of the installation photos is a visual statement that reveals their interpretation of space's physical and social aspects. Portrayed in the installation photographs, the images of the research sites were repeated several times in the form of a photographic series, where the photograph's subject was the photograph itself. These reflective images of the exhibition space provided a bridge between the numerous exploration sites and the online environment, enabling additional reading for the digital exhibition's visitors.

As we have already left the pandemic behind, a re-evaluation of the success and shortcomings of the course method remains necessary to understand better the agency and potential of photography in architectural education. It is possible to mention two fundamental aspects of this pedagogical approach.

On the one hand, this method, with a focus on the restorative effect of the every day, can be revisited in any extraordinary circumstances that might deactivate or cause a profound change in the daily practices of the students or in the case of an urgent necessity of online education. Since the geographic context from where this pedagogical experience emerged, Turkey faced a massive earthquake that affected more than 11 cities and more than 13 million people who had to leave their hometowns as immigrants or live in temporary dwellings. Only one academic year after the students were back on campus, many had their every day paralysed again and experienced another form of a lockdown going back to online education. Therefore, the photographic method is valuable both in terms of healing and improving daily life and in creating an alternative plan that can provide students with an area of activism without architectural education's physical and social space. Feedback from course evaluation forms consistently highlighted the positive impact of iterative photographic writing on students' well-being throughout the semester. It also notably improved their analytical and interpretative skills, particularly in the architectural design studio.

On the other hand, in a broader context of architectural education, photography is a peculiar tool that translates and conveys the creative and critical writing skills of students from the literary field to the visual field, especially in an era where the production and circulation of digital images are a significant part of daily life. Different media have become both the communication and research tools of architecture. In today's world, where the importance of ecological thinking is undeniable and the intersection of environmental history and environmental humanities with the fields of architecture, planning, and design is intensifying, a photographic focus on the every day leads to ecological awareness, understanding the urban reality through the relations between human and non-human entities, including quotidian objects.

In parallel, photography is suggested to have an agency in an ecological understanding of the built environment that students are aiming to gain. This ecology includes their selves as participating observers on the everyday level they share with the coexisting others. Opened a field for amplification and discussion, the course is presented here as one reference point, which enables

116 Bilge Beril Kapusuz Balci

the reading of local and universal reflections on the parts and potentials of visual research and photographic writing and their complementary role to architectural design.

Notes

1 Albena Yaneva, "Choreographies for the Laboratorized City," Architectural Theory Review 24.2 (2020): 188.
2 Yaneva, 188.
3 Yaneva, 191.
4 Elizabeth Ellsworth, Places of Learning: Media, Architecture, Pedagogy. (New York: Routledge: 2005), 38.
5 Ellsworth,55.
6 Laura Sanderson and Sally Stone, Introduction to Emerging Practices in Architectural Pedagogy: Accommodating an Uncertain Future (New York: Routledge, 2021), 3.
7 Sanderson and Stone, 4.
8 In 2020–2021 Spring Semester, 28 students were enrolled, and 27 of them contributed to the course M3802 Image Construction and Architectural Photography and submitted their final works, names of whom are listed here: Yaşanur Çil, Ömer Faruk Ormancı, Seda Nur Abat, Yunus Emre Akdemir, Feyza Akman, Zehra Betül Alkılınç, Sümeyye Atasayar, Ferdanur Cihan, Zeynep Coşkuner, Özge Çelebi, Eren Burak Çöplü, Feyza Gül Ekim, Mehmet Eroğlu, Şevval Güner, Ayşe Nur Haldan, Berfin Kangal, Sait Kızıl, Gözde Külfetoğlu, Dilannur Özdemir, Mervenur Öztürk, Erol Üresin, Fikriye Merve Yıldız, Anıl Yücesan, Hüseyin Avni Halıcı, Burhan Çakmak, Aleyna Çakır, and Alperen Sürmeneli. I would like to thank all my students for their enthusiasm, curiosity, effort, and brilliant contributions in this extraordinary situation.
9 Albena Yaneva. "Politics of architectural imaging: Four ways of assembling a city," in Elements of Architecture: Assembling Archaeology, Atmosphere and the Performance of Building Spaces, eds. Mikkel Bille and Tim Flohr Sorensen. (New York: Routledge, 2016.), 238.
10 Yaneva, 239.
11 Yaneva, 241.
12 Albena Yaneva, Mapping Controversies in Architecture (New York: Routledge, 2016), 108.
13 Bruno Latour and Albena Yaneva, "Give me a gun and I will make all buildings move: An ANT's view of architecture," in Explorations in Architecture: Teaching, Design, Research, ed. Reto Geiser (Basel: Birkhäuser,2008), 80–89.
14 Jeremy Till, Architecture Depends (Cambridge: The MIT Press, 2009), 95.
15 Eduardo Cadava, Words of light: Theses on the Photography of History (Princeton: Princeton University Press, 2018), xvii.
16 Richard Shusterman, "Photography as a Performative Process." The Journal of Aesthetics and Art Criticism 70.1 (2012): 67.
17 Ian Wiblin, "Photography, Performance, Ruin: Performing Photography in Site of Architecture." Performance Research 20.3 (2015): 126.
18 Wiblin, 129.
19 Selay Yurtkuran Tok et al., "Photography in Architectural Education: A Tool for Assessing Social Aspects of the Built Environment." Procedia-Social and Behavioral Sciences 2.2 (2010): 2583.
20 Abeer Elshater, "The Power of Photography in Urban Design Discipline: A Module Catalogue." International Journal of Architectural Research: ArchNet-IJAR 12.2 (2018): 182–208. doi:10.26687/ARCHNET-IJAR.V12I2.1594.

21 Pedro Neto et al., "From a Pedagogical Experience of a Photography Course on Architectural and Public Space into a Research Project focused on Communication of Public Space's State and Evolution, Architecture and Urban Cultures." EUNIS 2012: A 360° perspective on IT/IS in Higher Education (2012). https://hdl.handle.net/10216/64757

22 Annalisa Trentin et al., "Curating the City." European Journal of Creative Practices in Cities and Landscapes 3.1 (2020): 3.

23 Sarah Chaplin and Alexandra Stara. *Introduction to Curating Architecture and the City* (New York: Routledge, 2009), 2.

24 The virtual environment of the course, the digital exhibition space, can be accessed on the grid of the Instagram account: imageconstruction_2019. https://www.instagram.com/imageconstruction_2019/

25 A passage from the text of the student Hüseyin Avni Halıcı on his work entitled "Confusion":

[...]I chose a park-wide across a sidewalk and focused on a concrete object that divides the walkway into two, right in the middle of the area designed as a walking path. I realised with this work that something I used to pass by every day was a pond. Perhaps this artefact, which has never been filled with water since the day it was built, is now used by people only as a resting place while passing by. Perhaps this pool, made with an aesthetic concern, has taken its function to a completely different dimension and has become more beneficial to people. One of the things I question here is, which state of this structure, away from its purpose and function to such a degree, is a more helpful service?

26 A passage from the text of the student Zeynep Coşkuner on her work entitled "The Square: The Heart":

These changes were seen in the time frame in which the frame was photographed and reflected in the exhibition[...]Hundreds of people use the square every day for different purposes. In almost every photograph, these people become a story in the frame [...]. So many elements are the subject of the photographs that they all contain a different story. However, the most exciting image is the sweet pigeons chasing the small breadcrumbs of the square's residents and following the sweet rush of the pigeons and the breadcrumbs flying around the people who approach them, disappearing at some times of the day but constantly differentiating the frame. As you can see, the square is the city's heart, not only for people but also for animals. The square was used as a point of emphasis in the frame created. When looking at the frame, the focus is on the square, which is a warm environment in the heart of a small city [...] The element that creates the desire to go and photograph with the same enthusiasm for 30 days is the effect of the changing lights and clouds in the sky every hour. The aim was to go in the morning one day and see the redness of the sky at sunset the next day. Furthermore, it is a flock of pigeons whose future is uncertain.

27 A passage from the text of the student Eren Burak Çöplü on his work entitled "Crossroads":

The "Crossroads" project, which was implemented with the idea of seeing the intersection space and its users, which was tried to be achieved while determining the frame and including the weather conditions (by duplicating the sky) into the frame. After 20 photographs were taken, it turned into a reality. When the photographs are examined one after the other, the changes in the space and the variety, cycles and density of users can be discussed in different directions and conclusions. Installation of the photographs as a stripe on the edge of the sidewalk disrupted the analysed cycles when the people stopped to see what was there.

28 A passage from the text of the student Dilannur Özdemir on her work entitled "Mirror mirror on the wall:

who is the fastest city of them all?" The city is changing/transforming every moment with all of its assets [...]The city contains transformation and variation in every part of it[...] The existing façade was influential in determining the framing. With the reflective effect of the façade, the city's cycle was followed. This fragment of the city was observed at different times on different days. The eye that looks at the city and constructs the frame is also a part of the fragment in which the subject accompanies the change. It is sometimes erased from the frame by the effect of light, and sometimes, it is the focus of the fragment produced.

29 A passage from the text of the student Yaşanur Çil on her work entitled "Gap":

What was observed during the emergence of the project and reflected in the project itself is how limited and short-term the uses of this in-between space are. It can be said that the space, which is used only by children for playing and as a parking lot for a few cars at certain times, reflects the monotonous life of the people in general. It is possible to see the same dull pattern in the use of balconies, too. Balconies are generally used for daily needs, hanging laundry, etc. As a result of this observation process, while these little public spaces between buildings have the potential to live, they become idle in this increasingly lonely world.

Bibliography

Cadava, Eduardo. *Words of Light: Theses on the Photography of History*. New Jersey: Princeton University Press, 2018.
Chaplin, Sarah, and Alexandra Stara. Introduction to *Curating Architecture and the City*, 1–6, New York: Routledge, 2009.
Ellsworth, Elizabeth. *Places of Learning: Media, Architecture, Pedagogy*. New York: Routledge, 2005.
Elshater, Abeer. "The Power of Photography in Urban Design Discipline: A Module Catalogue." International Journal of Architectural Research: ArchNet-IJAR 12.2 (2018): 182–208. doi:10.26687/ARCHNET-IJAR.V12I2.1594.
Latour, Bruno, and Albena Yaneva. "Give me a gun and I will make all buildings move: An ANT's view of architecture." In *Explorations in Architecture: Teaching, Design, Research*, edited by Reto Geiser, 80–89. Basel: Birkhäuser, 2008.
Neto, Pedro, et al. "From a Pedagogical Experience of a Photography Course on Architectural and Public Space into a Research Project focused on Communication of Public Space's State and Evolution, Architecture and Urban Cultures." *EUNIS 2012: A 360° perspective on IT/IS in Higher Education* (2012). https://hdl.handle.net/10216/64757
Sanderson, Laura, and Sally Stone. Introduction to *Emerging Practices in Architectural Pedagogy: Accommodating an Uncertain Future*, 1–15. New York: Routledge, 2021.
Shusterman, Richard. "Photography as Performative Process." The Journal of Aesthetics and Art Criticism. 70.1 (2012): 67–77.
Till, Jeremy. *Architecture Depends*. Cambridge: The MIT Press, 2009.
Trentin, Annalisa, Anna Rosellini, and Amir Djalali. "Curating the City." European Journal of Creative Practices in Cities and Landscapes. 3.1 (2020): 1–8.
Yaneva, Albena. "Choreographies for the Laboratorized City." Architectural Theory Review. 24.2 (2020): 188–191.

Yaneva, Albena. *Mapping Controversies in Architecture*. New York: Routledge, 2016.
Yaneva, Albena. "Politics of architectural imaging: Four ways of assembling a city." In *Elements of Architecture: Assembling Archaeology, Atmosphere and the Performance of Building Spaces*, edited by Mikkel Bille and Tim Flohr Sorensen, 238–255. New York: Routledge, 2016.
Yurtkuran Tok, Selay, Ian Kaplan, and Yavuz Taneli. "Photography in Architectural Education: A Tool for Assessing Social Aspects of the Built Environment." Procedia- Social and Behavioral Sciences. 2.2 (2010): 2583–2588.

Index

Note: Page numbers in *italics* refer to figures. Page numbers followed by "n" refer to notes.

Abrons, E. 74
abstract expressionism (art informel) 58
abstract painting (cubism) 58
actor–network theory (ANT) 105, 106
aesthetic communication theories 58
AI *see* artificial intelligence (AI)
aidagara (betweenness) 21
Alberti, L. B.: on façade 71
ANT *see* actor–network theory (ANT)
anthropology: definition of 22n9; digital 3, 11, 12, 21
AR *see* augmented reality (AR)
architectural conservation 1, 78
architectural treatise 57
artificial intelligence (AI) 2, 5, 29, 38, 39; code 57–61; column 67–68, *68*; dataset curation 62–64; disciplinary treatise, influence of 57; façade 71–73, *72*, *73*; integrated parametric three-dimensionalisation 65–67; language 57–61; pedagogy 4, 56–75; poor images 60–61, *60*; poorly trained models 61, *63*; portico 69–71, *69*, *70*
Ashton, K. 13
augmented reality (AR) 14
Augmented Studio 2, 9–21; 'Augmented Studio – A Manifesto, The' 17–21, *20*; digital dialectics 11–12; Metaverse 13–14, 21; 'push button' education 10–11; scenario 10
Avery Architectural and Fine Arts Library: Digital Serlio Project 62

Bacon, F.: on involuntary free marks 61; painting 58–59, *59*; on scrambled zones 58, *59*
BBC *see* British Broadcasting Corporation (BBC)
BIM 31, 32
Bluteau, J. M. 12
British Broadcasting Corporation (BBC) 11
Brown, J. B. 15
Buvat, J. 29

Cadava, E. 105, 107
Campus Water Utility Prediction App 41
canonical five orders 5
Carpo, M. 73
Carter, E.: voxel stacking *72*
ChatGPT4 29
Çil, Y. *114*; "Gap" 118n29
City of Rotterdam 25
columns, orthographic representations of 67–68, *68*
Çöplü, E. B. *113*; "Crossroads" 117n27
Coşkuner, Z. *109*, *112*; "Square: The Heart, The" 117n26
CT scans 67, *67*
curating 7, 102, 109–114
"Cure for the Self/City" 109–114, *111*–*114*
CyArk 80

data governance 3, 25, 27
dataset curation 62–64

Index 121

Deleuze, G. 5, 57–58; aesthetic communication theories 58; on asignifying traits 61
Design Studio 9, 15, 20
digital anthropology 3, 11, 12, 21
digital competence 3, 31
digital dialectics 11–12
Digital Heritage Preservation 79–81
digital intelligence 25–28; shared 3, 25, *37*
digital literacy 4, 29, 32
digital maturity 26, 30
digital skills 3, 4, 25–30, 39; broad-spectrum 32–38; in built environment pedagogy, value of 45–48; cross-disciplinary 44; hard 29, 31; soft 29, 31
digital talent development in built environment, uncoordinated 31
digital talent gap 3, 26, 28–30; in built environment 30–31, 46–48
digital twin (DT) 2, 14, 22n19
digital twin cities (DTCs) 3–4, 25–48; definition of 27–28; digital talent gap *see* digital talent gap; future of 28–30; Hatfield Digital Twin City Initiative, City of Tshwane, South Africa *see* Hatfield Digital Twin City Initiative, City of Tshwane, South Africa; uncoordinated digital talent development in built environment 31; as vehicles for redefining value of digital skills 45–48
Digital Twin Cities Centre, Sweden 27
DSLRs (Digital Single-Lens Reflex) camera 85
DT *see* digital twin (DT)
DTCs *see* digital twin cities (DTCs)
Dutton, T. A. 15

École des Beaux-Arts 74
Ellsworth, E.: *Places of Learning: Media, architecture, pedagogy* 104
Elshater, A. 108
Expanded Studio 2, 10, 19; furniture, re-arranging 14–17; global classroom *17*; interaction *16*; modelmaking workshops *16*; time 17–18; timetabling 17–18
experimental spaces of pedagogical process 12
Extraordinario Libro 69

façade 71–73, *72, 73*; waterfront 97
figurative resemblances (optical space of representation) 58
Fure, A. 74

gamification 20
GANs *see* generative adversarial networks (GANs)
Gazi University: "Image Construction and Architectural Photography" 7
GCPs *see* ground control points (GCPs)
generative adversarial networks (GANs) 5, 59, 66; architecture diagram *60*; layered 64–65, *65*; poor images 60–61, *60*; poorly trained AI model 61
GeoBIM 32
Geographic Information System (GIS) 34
GIS *see* Geographic Information System (GIS)
ground control points (GCPs) 89–90, *90*

Halıcı, H. A. *111*; "Confusion" 117n25
Hatfield Alternative Net-Zero Urban Energy 41
Hatfield Digital Twin City Initiative, City of Tshwane, South Africa 4, 27, 32–46, *33*; broad-spectrum digital skills development 32, 34–38, *35, 37*; high-end technological solutions 38–41, *39, 40*; shared digital talent, building 43–45, *45*; transdisciplinary works 41–43, *42, 43*; Vertical Studio 38
Hatfield Zero-Waste Project 41, *42*
Horst, H. 11

"Image Construction and Architectural Photography" course, Gazi University's Faculty of Architecture 101, 103
immediate environment, as expanded field/space of pandemic everyday/learning 105–107
integrated parametric three-dimensionalisation 65–67
interior design 1
interior scans, visualisation of 91
Internet of Spaces (IoS) 9, 13, 14, 21
Internet of Things (IoT) 9, 13, 14, 32
IoS *see* Internet of Spaces (IoS)
IoT *see* Internet of Things (IoT)

Index

Krueger, J. 21

Lady Bird Johnson Wildflower Center 6, 89, *89*; plan drawings 92
Latour, B. 7, 102, 107; actor–network theory 105, 106
layered GANs 64–65, *65*
LeanBIM 31
LiDAR *see* Light Detection and Ranging (LiDAR) scans
Light Detection and Ranging (LiDAR) scans 81, 82, 85–87

machine learning (ML) 38, 39, 74; networks 5, 59
Massive Open Online Course (MOOC) 11
Melusi Climate Adaption Studio *39*, *46*
Metaverse 3, 13–14, 21
Middlesex University 19; Interior Architecture 14–15, *14*
Miller, D. 11, 12, 22n9
ML *see* machine learning (ML)
modulation 58
module 58
MOOC *see* Massive Open Online Course (MOOC)

Neto, P. L. 108

oculus 92, *92*
OpenStreetMap 36
Open University, UK 10–11
Osler, L. 21
Özdemir, D. *113*; "Mirror mirror on the wall" 118n28

pedagogy 15, 31, 45–48; AI 4, 56–75; of alternative daily routine 104–109; point cloud 2, 5–6, 78–97; signature 9, 18
photogrammetry 2, 6, 78–80, 82–88, 92–94, 96
photographic writing 101–118; as pedagogical tool 107–109, *109*
plan drawings 92, 94
point cloud pedagogy 2, 5–6, 78–97; 3D Laser Scan Point Cloud, visualisation of 90, *91*; animation 90; art of 87–88; Building C of Seaholm Intake Building 97, *97*; camera position 96; challenges in the field 84–87; cloud render 96; definition of 78; detail, finding 83–84; Digital Heritage Preservation 79–81; drawing set 94, *95*; ground control points 89–90, *90*; independent field study 81–82; interior perspective 97; interior scans, visualisation of 91; Lady Bird Johnson Wildflower Center 89, *89*; oculus 92, *92*; parts 91; plan drawings 92, 94; post-pandemic teaching 87; rendered 3D mesh 91–92; section breakaway 96; section drawings 93–94, *93*; vignettes 90; waterfront façade 97
poor images 60–61
poorly trained models 61, *63*
portico 69–71, *69*, *70*
post-pandemic teaching 87
Price, C.: *National School Plan, The* 11
procedural generation 65–66
'push button' education 10–11

Ramo, S. 11
"Realty Capture for Architecture," University of Texas, Austin, School of Architecture 79, 89, *89–91*, *95*, *96*
Rendell, J. 12
rendered 3D mesh 91–92

Safe Space 20
Sanabria, L.: voxel stacking *68*
Sanderson, L.: *Emerging Practices in Architectural Pedagogy: Accommodating an Uncertain Future* 104–105
Schön, D.: *Reflective Practitioner, The* 15
Scott, J.: encoded patterns *67*; UV mapping *66*; voxel stacking *66*, *68*
Seaholm Intake Building 6, 94; Building C 97, *97*
section drawings 93–94, *93*
Serlio, S. 56–57, 62–65, *63*, 73, 75; on altered object status 62; column images *67*, *68*; façade images 71; portico images 69, *70*; *Tvtte l'opera d'architettvra, et prospetiva* (All the Works on Architecture and Perspective) 57
shared intelligence 4, 56, 62
signature pedagogy 9, 18
Sinanan, J. 12
sinGAN 64; portico 69, *69*

Index 123

smart cities 28
Stephenson, N.: *Snow Crash* 13
styleGAN 64, *65*; columns 67; façade 71; portico 69, *69*

thick time 106–107
3D Laser Scan Point Cloud, visualisation of 90, *91*
3D point cloud model 79, 80, 83, 85–87
3D point-cloud-to-GeoBIM models 41
3D laser scanning 2, 6, 78, 85, 87, 89–94, *91*, 96, 97
Till, J. 106
Tok, S. Y. 108

UAVs *see* Unmanned Aerial Vehicles (UAVs)
ultraviolet (UV) mapping 66, *66*, 70; columns 67–68; façade 72; portico 70
Unmanned Aerial Vehicles (UAVs) 6, 81, 82, 85, 87, 89, 97
urban planning 1, 2; revolutionising 3
urban sustainability 28
use-case 41

Vertical Studio 38
vertical studio 18

virtual learning environment (VLE) 10, 19
virtual reality (VR) 12, 13, 14
Virtual Singapore 27
VLE *see* virtual learning environment (VLE)
VO (Visual Observer) 87
voxelisation 66
voxel stacking *66*; columns 67–68, *68*; façade 71, *72*
VR *see* virtual reality (VR)

Water Intake Structure, Lady Bird Lake, Austin, TX 94
water twin 41
Watsuji, T. 21
WEF *see* World Economic Forum (WEF)
Wellington Digital Twin City 27
White, A. 73
Wiblin, I. 108
Wilson, H. 10
World Economic Forum (WEF): Future of Jobs 2020 Report 29
Writing Portfolio 18

Yaneva, A. 7, 105–107; "Choreographies for the Laboratorized City" 102–103
Young, S.: portico images *69*, *70*

For Product Safety Concerns and Information please contact our EU representative GPSR@taylorandfrancis.com
Taylor & Francis Verlag GmbH, Kaufingerstraße 24, 80331 München, Germany

www.ingramcontent.com/pod-product-compliance
Lightning Source LLC
Chambersburg PA
CBHW051753230426
43670CB00012B/2263